"For many evangelicals, church his ts,
has a brief stopover in the Protestar   e
present day. In *Church History for N*   s
our dangerous a-historical view by n   .1.
I'll be recommending this to pastors ¿   ....ers alike. It's a great
way for them to meet the family they never knew they had!"

—Drew Dyck, managing editor, *Leadership Journal*;
author, *Yawning at Tigers: You Can't Tame God, So Stop Trying*

"Hartman gives us an enjoyable, readable, and trustworthy book that
helps us see the theological and ministerial value of studying our history. If you're a pastor, you need to know church history—not just for
doctrinal clarity and sermon illustrations, but also for your own spiritual nourishment. I will be pointing pastors and aspiring pastors to this
book for years to come."

—Tony Merida, PhD; Johnny Hunt Chair of Biblical Preaching,
Southeastern Baptist Theological Seminary

"It seems to me that 95 percent of the stupid things we do as pastors
could be avoided if we knew a little church history. I am very happy
that Dayton Hartman has written this book. As both a practicing pastor and a practicing church historian, he is well poised to bring the insights of our forefathers to bear on the day-to-day issues that confront
church leaders. That *Church History for Modern Ministry* is both short
and snarky is an added bonus!"

—Mike McKinley, author; contributor and speaker, 9Marks;
senior pastor, Sterling Park Baptist Church (Sterling, VA)

"In this helpful book Hartman shows pastors why we should appreciate church history. Every generation of Christians and pastors stands
on the shoulders of those who have gone before. The lessons that God
taught our forebears can be very useful for ministry today. Hartman
helps us see how this is so, and also provides practical suggestions for
introducing historical insights into congregational life. I recommend
this book for pastors as well as other church leaders."

—Tom Ascol, PhD; executive director, Founders Ministries

"Christians in America today—especially evangelicals—suffer from a damaging lack of connection to the 'cloud of witnesses' who have preceded us in Christian history. I am happy to commend Dr. Dayton Hartman's readable introduction to church history for pastors, who will surely be the key players in teaching Christians about the riches of the church's past."

—Thomas S. Kidd, PhD; professor of history, Baylor University

"Over the past decade, I have taught church history to over a thousand seminarians and college students. Many of them have raised questions about whether or not church history is really useful for pastors and other ministers. While I make regular pastoral application in the classroom, I have yet to find a good book to point students to that weds church history and practical ministry. I'm grateful that pastor-historian Dayton Hartman has written this book—it fills an important gap and answers many of the questions my students are asking. I hope *Church History for Modern Ministry* is widely read and leads more pastors and other ministry leaders to mine the depths of Christian history for contemporary spiritual flourishing."

—Nathan Finn, PhD; dean of the School of Theology and Missions, Union University

"All pastors and Christian teachers can greatly benefit from a solid knowledge of church history. And the best place to start is with Dayton Hartman's book *Church History for Modern Ministry*. This helpful book presents the key content of church history in a clear, concise, and careful manner. Yet the book is also distinct in reflecting careful theological ideas in a readable and sometimes humorous way. I endorse this book and its author to all readers."

—Kenneth R. Samples, senior research scholar, Reasons to Believe

"*Church History for Modern Ministry* is a lighthearted yet serious look into the value of Christian history for contemporary ministry. Knowing the past helps ministers respond to future events with practical wisdom and theological depth. Hartman frames historical and theological developments with the expertise of a historian and the disposition of a pastor while introducing us to saints of old along the way."

—Walter Strickland II, special advisor to the president
for diversity, instructor of theology,
Southeastern Baptist Theological Seminary

"Cloaked in skinny jeans, coiffed with a faux-hawk, and possessed by a sense of humor and engaging style, Dayton Hartman invites his tribe (pastors) to visit the foreign country that is the church's past. An able guide, Hartman gives an introductory tour that will surely inspire his group to visit again and again and to appreciate, value, and dialogue with church history as they press on to lead the people of God today."

—Edward L. Smither, PhD; dean of the College of Intercultural
Studies, Columbia International University;
author of *Augustine as Mentor*

"This book is like most of my favorite books: short, enjoyable, and surprisingly practical! Hartman has provided an easy-to-read primer on the need and relevance of church history for our modern-day ministry. This book is anything but dry, and Hartman writes in a way that is relatable, refreshingly accessible, and immediately helpful. I was challenged by my own distance from the church of the past and encouraged to close that gap as a result of this work. Read it, enjoy it, and put these exhortations to use for the glory of God and the good of His church!"

—Brian Davis, hip-hop artist (God's Servant),
Lamp Mode Recordings; pastor/church planter,
Risen Christ Fellowship (Philadelphia, PA)

CHURCH
HISTORY
FOR MODERN
MINISTRY

CHURCH HISTORY FOR MODERN MINISTRY

Why Our Past Matters for Everything We Do

DAYTON HARTMAN

LEXHAM PRESS

Church History for Modern Ministry: Why Our Past Matters for Everything We Do

Copyright 2016 Dayton Hartman

Lexham Press, 1313 Commercial St., Bellingham, WA 98225
LexhamPress.com

Print ISBN 9781577996606
Digital ISBN 9781577997009

Lexham Editorial Team: Rebecca Brant, Lynnea Fraser, Abigail Stocker
Cover Design: Christine Gerhart
Back Cover Design: Brittany Schrock
Typesetting: ProjectLuz.com

To my children:

Thank God for what has been and trust God for what will be.

CONTENTS

ACKNOWLEDGMENTS

I owe a debt of gratitude to Brannon Ellis for his belief in this project and to Todd Hains for refining its content. Also, to my wife for her willingness to be my sounding board and first-draft editor. In addition, I'm very grateful to Josh Wester and Erik Harris for providing chapter-by-chapter feedback. By God's grace, these collective efforts will make this material useful to my readers.

1

BACK TO THE FUTURE

"Martin Luther was a chump." Yes, I said it. I used to believe it. In fact, reflecting on my early adulthood, I had the nastiest case of chronological snobbery I've seen outside of KJV-only circles.

So what if Martin Luther (1483–1546) ignited the Reformation? Who cares that he preached a biblical gospel? Today many evangelicals consider much of Luther's thought to be in error, or at least in poor taste. Worse yet, although he was arguably one of the greatest theologians of his time, the most average of theologians today seems undeniably superior.

Why? Well, we have Logos Bible Software, and Together for the Gospel conferences, and we can live tweet major theological events. Who live-tweeted the posting of the Ninety-Five Theses? Nobody! That's probably a good thing. Can you imagine the hashtags #IFixedYourDoctrine or #TetzelFail? Those would be the tamest. When angry, Luther's vocabulary was less Dr. Phil and more Lewis Black. Since Luther's revolution was neither televised nor live tweeted, it obviously has little value, except for that whole defending the gospel thing.

Not until I had spent a full year in pastoral ministry did I begin to see the value of what has come before. I remember wrestling with my own explanations of the relationship between the gospel and works. Then I started looking more closely at Luther's works to see what this "old timer" said in error. I was shocked that, rather than being amused by Luther's errors, I was overwhelmed by his insight. Luther's wrestling was, in a sense, my wrestling. Luther's pastoral burden to preach grace to his church was, and is, my burden. Still, even after accepting and embracing the theological riches of Reformation leaders, I maintained my disdain for the early church fathers and the creeds they helped form. After all, those Catholics love creeds, and they revere many of the early church fathers. Therefore, creeds and the church fathers must be useless to me as a Protestant pastor.

As I delved more deeply into apologetic writings, however, I latched onto Francis Schaeffer (1912–1984), only to see that he occasionally referenced the early church fathers. Even though Schaeffer's thought changed my life, I dismissed his occasional church history references as proof that "nobody is perfect."

Chronological Snobbery

The assumption that the current intellectual culture is inherently superior to any previous period. Thus, old is bad.

Martin Luther (1483–1546)

This Augustinian monk ignited the Protestant Reformation through his Ninety-Five Theses (1517) and his argument that salvation is God's gracious gift, received by faith alone in Christ alone.

Francis Schaeffer (1912–1984)

This American evangelical became widely known for his unique blend of Christian apologetics, cultural assessments, and Reformed theology. Schaeffer moved to Switzerland where he established the renowned L'Abri Community.

Then I began to engage Mormons and Muslims in my community. The claims that they made about church history shook me. In response, I decided to scrutinize their accusations against the first Christians.

I dove headlong into the early church fathers. I embraced this new direction in research so completely that I purchased Philip Schaff's (1819–1893) massive 38-volume set of translated early church works.[1] It was incredibly cumbersome to use, but it looked amazing on a bookshelf. Just having it in my office made me feel—and probably look—smarter. As I made my way through this series, I found that my Mormon and Muslim friends were sorely mistaken in their understanding of early church history—and that I was too.

The early church fathers were incredibly helpful. Instead of seeming strange and foreign, they seemed familiar and welcoming. I was surprised by how much Justin Martyr's (100–165) apologetic writings applied to our culture. I was moved by the seriousness with which Augustine (354–430) undertook efforts to disciple young people. I found myself at home among early Christians, struggling to hold onto biblical doctrine while striving to express it clearly.

In short, this multi-year journey into church history changed my view of the creeds, preaching, discipleship, pastoral care, and cultural engagement. I am a different and, I believe, better pastor because of church history. Now, more than a decade since my first foray into church history, I am a church planter. I also teach church history and historical theology to seminary students.

By wrestling with church history, I have identified a number of dangers inherent to ignoring the past, as well as many benefits to knowing what has come before us. These benefits have convinced me that pastoral ministry is maximally effective only if carried out in light of lessons from our history. Before moving into some of the practical benefits of knowing church history, let's look at how unfamiliarity with church history can cause dangerous error in doctrine and practice.

IGNORANCE IS DOCTRINALLY DANGEROUS

Throughout the *Back to the Future* series, Marty McFly, a hapless teenager, continually saves the present, and the future, by going back to the past in his DeLorean. While the series didn't help anyone understand anything about science (still, how cool is a flux capacitor?), there is one valuable takeaway: The past was once the present, and the present is what dictates the future. For Christian theology, this is an invaluable reminder.

For pastors, ignoring the past is both foolish and dangerous. During my first stop in vocational ministry, I met a young man who had only recently been called to his first pastorate. Over the next two years, I watched as this young, uneducated preacher moved from a shallow orthodoxy into the deep waters of heresy. As he preached week-in and week-out, he began to "see" things in the text of Scripture that led him to believe that Jesus was created by the Father. He began to embrace heresies condemned long ago as unscriptural.

In his mind, he had found something that no one else had ever found before; he was the next great theologian. But in reality, he was simply another hack heretic who would hurt believers and eventually drop out

Philip Schaff

A German Reformed historian, Schaff was one of the most prolific church historians of his day. He served as a professor at Union Theological Seminary (New York).

Christological Controversies

During the fourth and fifth centuries, Christians debated the deity and humanity of Christ. Some heretics argued that Christ was created by the Father (Arianism); others divided his divine and human natures into two persons (Nestorianism); others conflated his divine and human natures (Eutychianism). Through the convocation of four ecumenical councils—Nicaea (325), Constantinople (381), Ephesus (431), and Chalcedon (451)—the church affirmed that Jesus is true God, sharing the same essence with the Father and the Spirit, and that his divine and human natures are distinguishable but inseparable in the unity of his person.

of ministry. Looking back, I wonder how a little knowledge of church history could have prevented his errors. What if he had been aware of the christological controversies in the early church and the orthodox response to the claims he was making? I believe he would still be in the ministry.

IGNORANCE IS PROBLEMATIC FOR POLITY

For many pastors, ignoring church history will not lead to theological errors regarding the deity of Christ, but it can lead to many practical errors. For much of my undergraduate education, I assumed that a democratically elected board of deacons who served in three-year terms led all churches throughout history. I was utterly floored the first time I found out that this was not the norm throughout Christian history—not even in my Southern Baptist tradition. I was shocked to learn that elders and deacons were not the same thing and that there were churches that took seriously both the distinctions between these roles and the biblical qualifications assigned to these offices. I began to rethink these matters, not because of a new approach to exegesis but because of history. These distinctions long existed, and the biblical qualifications for these roles mattered.

Exegesis

The critical explanation or interpretation of a scriptural text.

Through this exploration I discovered that most Christians go through life with incredible historical bias and prejudice without realizing it. For instance, as an American, I assumed that democracy is a "Christian" thing and that churches have always practiced this form of government. I was wrong. I found that many, including my own tradition, had formerly practiced a much more biblical form of church government—elder-led congregationalism.

Moreover, as I began to examine the historical distinctions that led to the current state of my own tradition, I found out that Southern

Baptists were not always deacon-led, democratic congregationalists who hate dancing and syncopated rhythms. Instead, ours is a tradition that emphasizes baptism by immersion, religious liberty, regenerate church membership, and biblical authority (among other distinctives). History led me to understand that I was not a Baptist by tradition, but by conviction. Tradition that lacks biblical conviction can only lead to error. Convictions informed by traditions protect against error.

Congregational Rule

In this model of church government, the congregation has the final authority—under the direction of the Scriptures—in matters of doctrine and church discipline. In its most biblically faithful form, a plurality of elders or pastors lead. However, some congregations, which misconstrue the biblical precedence for congregational rule, practice a form of governance far more indebted to American democracy than to the Bible.

This principle is incredibly important. It's now a matter of public record that denominations are in decline. Most millennials find denominational affiliation problematic. One impetus for this disdain of denominations arises from a misunderstanding regarding the purpose of denominations. In my experience, most Baptists aren't sure why they are Baptist. This alone would be bad enough, but many pastors in various traditions also aren't entirely sure why they align with the denomination in which they find themselves.

I am convinced, pastors, that if you became aware of the historical-theological basis for your denominational tradition, you would either jump ship or become reinvigorated in your support for your tradition. If you are passionate for your tradition, many in your congregations will be as well. Stories shape our lives. Our traditions have a story to tell. It's time we hear those stories and tell those stories.

WHY CHURCH HISTORY?

Aside from avoiding the fallacy of chronological snobbery, church history is essential to pastoral ministry because of its benefits. Knowing and communicating church history through your words, actions, ministry, and liturgy will produce a variety of healthy outcomes for your church body.

> ### Liturgy
>
> The consistent content, form, rhythms, and practices of worship.

Church history equips pastors and churches to address social issues.

For instance, church history helps us address issues of racial reconciliation. History enables us to view ourselves as part of a large, ethnically diverse family. As our nation continues to wrestle with the scars left by our racist history and shameful past in human slavery and trafficking, the church can lead in casting a vision for an ethnically diverse future.

In light of church history, we can emphasize that Christianity has always been an ethnically diverse family of faith. We actually have the only basis for genuine racial diversity: the gospel. Through Christ, the church is unified, but it is not uniform. Thus, church history does not narrate the struggles and successes of only one ethnicity or culture. Instead, we encounter people in various cultures in various places at various times: 4th- and 5th-century North African bishops, 12th-century French preachers, 16th-century German monks, 18th-century Anglo-American theologians, 20-century African-American and Latino social activists. This is strong medicine against chronological and cultural snobbery.

Church history supplies the tools and models necessary for healthy approaches to discipleship in the local church.

Christians, and specifically pastors, have always been concerned with making disciples. However, many evangelical churches in America systematically, and unintentionally, fail to disciple children and new believers well. Following the patterns of those who have come before us, we and our congregations can regain a biblical vision for making disciples (more on this in chapter 3).

Church history is useful for effectively proclaiming and preaching the gospel in cultures indifferent and even hostile to Christianity.

Every generation of pastors wrestles with how to communicate clearly in our preaching and how to faithfully engage the culture around us. Our generation is not the first to wrestle with the complexities of linguistic relevancy and cultural engagement. We would do well to draw from the deep 2,000-year-old well of wisdom. Our forebears were master expositors, fine cultural exegetes, and gifted orators. The wisdom they have handed down is of great value (more on this in chapter 4).

Church history enables us to critically assess culture as we resolve to create culture.

Throughout history, Christianity has been seen as subversive and threatening to emperors and empires. We profess citizenship in a heavenly kingdom, we see our churches as outposts of a that kingdom, and we declare allegiance to a heavenly King. Why, then, do we perpetuate Christian subcultures that repackage sanitized versions of what the prevailing culture of our day produces? Why do we not produce persuasive cultural products that reflect a kingdom culture? Is this what Christians have always done? Have we always preached a gospel that can redeem the world, but failed to produce redemption-reflecting culture that is good and worthwhile? There is a better way forward, and we see that way forward by looking to our past (more on this in chapter 5).

Church history serves as a road map from the present to the future.

The trajectory from the past to the present can provide a glimpse into the future. As we prepare for future years of ministry, continued examination of the past can help us foresee what will likely be the future of our churches and our ministries. Therefore, it is vital that every pastor create a plan for engaging church history.

ANCIENT TRUTH FOR NEW QUESTIONS

So many miss that Christian doctrine and practice have developed over time. This is not to say Christian doctrine was "invented" in stages. Rather, previous struggles and conflicts regarding doctrine and daily devotion have clarified ancient truths, refining and reforming our doctrine and practice today. Real world questions in a given period and place always shape Christian theology. The church must answer these new questions with ancient truths. Today, pastors and theologians are being asked to address questions on issues ranging from immigration and enculturation to transhumanism and the transgender community.

Transhumanism

A movement that seeks to "better" the human race through the augmentative integration of technology into human bodies.

Transgender

People who live out their gender identities differently from those who equate gender identity with biological sex (see Mark A. Yarhouse, *Understanding Gender Dysphoria* [Downers Grove, IL: IVP Academic, 2015], 20).

DEAR PASTOR,

How you address such questions and challenges will influence and even determine the contours of Christian theology and practice for generations to come. Your task is immense, but you have Scripture as your authority and 2,000 years of wisdom from those who have faithfully served, suffered, and persevered before you. I hope that this book will inspire you to embrace the value of church history. Those who have come and gone centuries and millennia before me have changed the way I do pastoral ministry today. In a sense, the dead discipled me and made me a better pastor. I pray they do the same for you!

ACTION STEPS

1. Identify and list historical blind spots in your educational background. What is your tradition's history? In which particular periods of church history do you have very little knowledge?

2. Pinpoint which periods or figures from church history most interest you. As you read this book, note the people and periods that most pique your curiosity. Throughout the book there are "extra information" sidebars that could spark your own research.

3. Take inventory of your ability to properly navigate the demands of pastoral ministry. Which elements of the ministry are most taxing on you? For what specific pastoral task do you feel ill-equipped?

4. Use each chapter's topics and suggested readings as a springboard for overcoming deficiencies (whether real or perceived) in your ministry.

REFLECTION QUESTIONS

1. What is "chronological snobbery"?

2. What are two areas of error that can occur because of unfamiliarity with church history?

3. What were the four ecumenical councils that addressed the deity of Christ?

4. What are the five ways that church history can benefit pastoral ministry and the life of the church?

5. How has church history affected your ministry?

6. Why should pastors study church history?

RECOMMENDED READING

Daniel Akin, *How to Build a Theological Library* (www.danielakin.com, 2013). I'd recommend this resource for anyone building a library. Akin lists the most beneficial volumes for research in each major category of Christian studies.

Jonathan Hill, *Zondervan Handbook to the History of Christianity* (Grand Rapids: Zondervan, 2006). This is your must-have guide to church history. Hill is a perfect companion for any novice explorer looking to plumb the depths of church history.

John D. Hannah, *The Kregel Pictorial Guide to Church History*, 6 vols. (Grand Rapids: Kregel, 2001–2011). Hannah's detailed timeline is helpful for distinguishing people and periods of church history. It's a great companion resource to any church history text.

Mark A. Noll, *Turning Points: Decisive Moments in the History of Christianity* (Grand Rapids: Baker Academic, 2012). This great resource for those seeking to understand the pivotal moments in church history. While not a survey of all church history, Noll's work offers a digestible and helpful overview for beginners.

Robert F. Rea, *Why Church History Matters: An Invitation to Love and Learn from Our Past* (Downers Grove, IL: InterVarsity Press, 2014). Rea's work is one of the finest for supplying an apologetic for the general usefulness of church history to the Christian life. Although not directly applicable to pastoral ministry, Rea's work helps readers develop a broad appreciation for the lessons of church history.

Ruth Tucker, *Parade of Faith: A Biographical History of the Christian Church* (Grand Rapids: Zondervan, 2011). Written primarily as a textbook, Tucker's work is a large collection of short biographies. For those seeking to understand not only the *what* of history, but also the *who*, Tucker's work is an excellent resource.

Robert C. Walton, *Chronological and Background Charts of Church History*, rev. ed. (Grand Rapids: Zondervan, 2005). If you are more of a visual learner, this resource (and its accompanying software) will help you understand the flow of church history.

2

CREED AND CREEDS

I'm not saying that Creed is the greatest band of all time, but they are. I was that guy who waited with bated breath for the announcement of each album. The first time I heard someone say "Nicene Creed," I thought it was some obscure single of theirs that I had never heard.

So I immediately fired up my browser and searched "Nicene Creed Song." Only one hit. I clicked "download." Two days later—remember dial-up?—the download completed. As soon as I clicked play, I realized my mistake. There was no guttural singing and no nu metal guitar. Instead, it was a bunch of guys chanting. It was weird, even foreign-sounding. Still, I kind of liked it.

I quickly learned that many Protestants have no use for the Nicene Creed, or any creed for that matter: Creeds seem to be a Roman Catholic phenomenon that violates the principle of *sola Scriptura*. As I researched and read these creeds, I found that they are succinct summaries of biblical orthodoxy.[1] In fact, most creeds were formulated in response to some heresy that was spreading through local churches. Rather than

Sola Scriptura

This doctrine teaches that Scripture is the final authority for Christian faith and practice. Closely related, Scripture—God-breathed, free from error, and true in all its affirmations—contains all that is necessary for salvation and holy living.

attempting to go beyond Scripture, the early creeds faithfully present accurate summaries of biblical orthodoxy that reflect *sola Scriptura*. Creeds act as orthodox guardrails for theologians and pastors.

Go Deeper: Heresy

Alister McGrath, *Heresy: A History of Defending the Truth* (New York: HarperOne, 2009).

Ben Quash and Michael Ward, eds., *Heresies and How to Avoid Them: Why It Matters What Christians Believe* (London: SPCK, 2007).

Lewis Ayres, *Nicaea and Its Legacy: An Approach to Fourth-Century Trinitarian Theology* (Oxford: Oxford University Press, 2004).

R. P. C. Hanson, *The Search for the Christian Doctrine of God: The Arian Controversy, 318–81* (Grand Rapids: Baker Academic, 2005).

FROM INNOVATION TO ERROR

While preparing for one of my first sermons, I was disappointed with the lack of creativity I found among many commentators. So the Sunday I preached, I tried to be innovative in my approach to the text. In hindsight, I wasn't innovative—I was disrespectful to the text and borderline blasphemous. After the sermon, a number of older congregants in the church offered obligatory words of encouragement.

Then it happened: One man dared to provide me with loving correction. I didn't receive it well at the time, but he was right. He said something like, "Son, I appreciate your passion and attempt to make Scripture relevant, but don't exceed what has come before you." His point? Self-righteous pride often leads to error. When pastors become theologically "creative," problems are sure to ensue. It's one thing to clarify and contextualize biblical orthodoxy; it is another thing to try to rewrite it.

Throughout church history, we find that some of the most notorious heretics were seemingly well-meaning pastors. For instance, Arius (250–336) was a pastor in Alexandria, Egypt. He was also one of the first pop artists; he publicized his teaching through rhyming chants and gained widespread popularity. Rather than continuing in the historic Christian belief that Jesus is the eternal Son of God, the second person of the Godhead, Arius taught that Jesus was created. The spread of Aruis' teaching led, in part, to the Council of Nicaea. The council fathers promulgated no new doctrine; instead, they reaffirmed historic Christian doctrine.

The legacy of Arius continues today in many churches. A recent LifeWay Research poll found that 16 percent of self-professed evangelicals believed that Jesus was created. Another 11 percent were unsure whether Jesus is eternal. And another 22 percent believed that God the Father is more "God" than Jesus.[2] Moreover, while 96 percent of those polled affirmed the doctrine of the Trinity, 51 percent denied that the Holy Spirit is a person. If you deny the personhood of the Spirit, you are not a Trinitarian. In short, old heresies, long condemned, abound among Christians.

Why? The problem is twofold. First, epidemically high percentages of the evangelical church are biblically illiterate. Second, many pastors are tragically unaware of past heresies. It might be cliché, but it's true for the local church: *Those who fail to learn from history are doomed to repeat it.* Many well-meaning pastors, trying to be creative or clear, preach heresy. I've often heard pastors attempt to explain the doctrine

---

Three Heresies

Modalism. This denies that the three persons of the Trinity are distinguishable but inseparable. Instead, God is one person, who reveals himself in different modes (e.g., Father, Son, and Spirit) throughout redemptive history. This is also known as Sabellianism.

Adoptionism. The belief that at some point during his earthly ministry, Jesus became the Son of God. This denies that Jesus is coeternal with the Father.

Docetism. This assumes that Jesus only *appeared* to be human. This denies that he was fully God and fully man.

---

of the Trinity by appealing to heresies like modalism or adoptionism. Even some of our hymns have docetic references and allusions (for example, the lyric "no crying he makes," from "Away in a Manger," doesn't sound like a fully human baby, does it?).

REBUILDING THE RAILS

What can be done to correct this lax attitude toward heresy? A good first step would be for us as pastors to embrace the orthodox summaries of Christian doctrine that have come from the past. Creeds are good gifts from our forebears in the faith. During the first centuries of church history, every defender of biblical orthodoxy was a pastor. Similarly, many of the worst heretics were also in some form of church leadership. Today, we rarely see the former, while we see the latter far too often.

So, if we are committed to *sola Scriptura*, how should we approach the creeds? I like to think of the relationship between Scripture and creeds as a highway.[3] Scripture is our starting point. It defines the direction and content of biblical orthodoxy. Our journey in biblical orthodoxy must take place within the lanes provided by Scripture. Within those lanes, Christians can disagree and remain on the safe road of biblical orthodoxy. Think of the lanes as different Christian traditions — Reformed, Wesleyan, or Charismatic, for example.

Guardrails — the creeds — protect those traveling along the highway of biblical orthodoxy. While allowing for diversity on non-essential issues, the creeds prevent us from veering off the highway of biblical orthodoxy. Because the safeguards exist, the only way to leave the safe road of orthodoxy is to do a great deal of damage. Biblical orthodoxy matters because God calls us to know and worship him as he has revealed himself through Scripture. When we fall into error or believe lies regarding the nature of God, our relationship with him suffers. It is critical that the people of God know and worship God in Spirit and Truth.

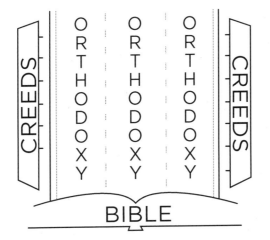

How can you put the creeds into practice as guardrails? First, you should familiarize yourself with the ecumenical creeds. Second, you should find creative ways to mention the creeds and their value in your sermons or Bible studies. Third, you should periodically recite creeds during worship.

PRACTICAL VALUE

Redeemer Church, where I serve as lead pastor, regularly makes use of the creeds during our worship gatherings. For example, if I am preaching on a passage with particular importance for establishing the doctrine of the incarnation, we will recite a creed or a section of a creed to provide a faithful summary of biblical orthodoxy concerning this doctrine. The benefits of incorporating the creeds into worship has amazed me.

First, reading creeds as part of worship has renewed our congregation's sense of the relationship we bear with the great cloud of witnesses: We are part of something ancient. Many faithful brothers and sisters have come before us, and many faithful brothers and sisters will come after us. Commenting on the origin of the creeds also combats our American-centric view of the Church. Each church is part of an ancient, global family of faith, not just its own denomination. Many American Christians tend to conflate American culture with biblical Christianity.

This attitude prevents some American Christians from recognizing the value of non-American theological contributions, hindering a deep appreciation for our brothers and sisters around the world. The acknowledgment that believers in the Middle East, Europe, Africa, and Asia contended for the faith long before the Americas were even discovered subtly counteracts implicit forms of racism and ethnocentrism. This global perspective should give birth to a celebratory attitude toward Christianity's expansion in the Global South and Asia. In short, reciting the creeds can contribute to racial reconciliation and a vision for the church drawn from every nation, tribe, and language.

Creeds and Confessions

What is the difference between creeds and confessions? Creeds are the guardrails of orthodoxy, while confessions detail the specifics of a tradition's theology. Most denominations have a specific confession or series of confessions that describe the core theological convictions of that tradition.

For example, the Southern Baptist Convention's (SBC) historic confession of faith is *The Abstract Principles* (1858). In 2000 the SBC published a new confession of faith, the *Baptist Faith and Message* (BFM2000). Our church periodically recites selections of BFM2000 and *The Abstract Principles* as part of worship. While these confessions are rather brief, many traditions use detailed confessions that address a wide breadth of secondary theological issues.

Second, introducing creeds into worship has matured our church body's theological literacy—a basic desire of all pastors. Scripture is full of theological phrases and ideas that are hard to understand without this knowledge. Creeds help tighten our theological vocabulary. You can equip your church members to do this in a variety of ways: through your preaching, through small group and Sunday school ministries, and through corporate readings. For instance, you could use holiday services or special occasions as opportunities to introduce creeds into a worship service. I have found corporate readings especially effective.

It is incredibly powerful to say these words together as a church. By explaining key terms prior to Scripture reading, you help the congregation use and understand basic but complex doctrines.

Finally, our church family has restored the value of the bounds of orthodoxy; we view heresy with grave seriousness. The pervasiveness of sub-biblical theologies in America should cause us great concern. Many evangelicals are confused about what biblical theology is. Some promote worldly blessings like health and wealth as the core of biblical faith. Others transform good things into ultimate things: freedom from oppression, fairer distribution of wealth, happiness, fulfillment, etc. All of these are good things, but they are not *the* good news. Often charismatic and inspiring people and messages are made more important than biblical orthodoxy.

BUT HOW?

Many pastors are reluctant to introduce changes into the life of the church, especially into worship. How will the congregation react? The church's leadership? "But that's how we've always done it," some might object. You need to recognize this fear. In some contexts, the order of weekly worship can be changed more quickly; in others, less so. You need to assess where your church is on this continuum.

Help your congregation understand that Scripture itself contains many creeds (for example, Deut 6:4; 1 Cor 8:6; 15:1–11; Phil 2:6–11). Introducing the congregation to creeds found within the text of Scripture can help your church become more comfortable with the concept of reciting creeds.

Churches can begin to include creeds as part of worship through a number of strategies. I would suggest the following approach. First, recite the Hebrew confession of monotheism, the *Shema* (Deut 6:4), and Paul's restatement of it in light of Christ's revelation (1 Cor 8:6). Then, during Holy Week, your congregation could read the Christ-centered hymn in Philippians 2 (vv. 6–11), as well as Paul's summary of the evidence of Christ's resurrection (1 Cor 15:1–11). Allow time in the service to explain these creeds. The congregation could then recite these creeds before learning others, like the Apostles' Creed or the Nicene Creed.

Catechism

A catechism organizes biblical truths into a series of questions and answers, often around the foundations of the Christian faith: the Our Father, the Creed, and the Ten Commandments (many included material about baptism, the Lord's Supper, and confession too). In the ancient church, new adult converts underwent a three-year process of catechesis. After finishing this process, they were baptized, usually on Easter, and added to the church membership.

One of the earliest Baptist catechisms for children is Henry Jesseynde's *A Catechism for Babes, or Little Ones* (1652).

The Gospel Coalition has created a convenient new catechism for families: the *New City Catechism* (www.newcitycatechism.com).

In addition, you could introduce creeds like the Apostles' Creed, the Nicene Creed, or the Athanasian Creed during special services or holiday gatherings. For instance, a communion service, which tends to have a greater sense of formality, is a very natural setting for reciting the Apostles' Creed. John Calvin (1509–1564) placed the creed before the Lord's Supper in his liturgy (in other liturgies the creed follows the sermon). Advent services also provide a good environment for using a creed, particularly the Nicene Creed. In celebrating the incarnation, draw attention to the second article of the creed, which affirms Jesus was born of a virgin. Then explain that the first Christians tightly connected the incarnation with the atonement. Why? The Nicene Creed immediately connects Christ's birth to Christ's work on the cross. This is also what the Apostle John had in mind when he encourages believers to test the spirits (1 John 4:1–6). Do those who profess faith in Jesus affirm that Jesus has come in the flesh, from God, for our redemption? Here the creeds provide an orthodox summary statement as a touchstone for John's prescription. In this worship context, noting this connection would transition seamlessly into preaching about the atonement.

DEAR PASTOR,

One of the most worthwhile results of corporate recitation of creeds is the sense of Christian unity it generates. That's the purpose of the creeds: to make us one in the faith. Guarding the bounds of orthodoxy, the creeds help us to see that everyone within the rails is our brother and sister. As Christianity becomes increasingly marginalized in our culture, unity across denominational lines (around gospel essentials) is increasingly important. A return to the creeds should renew the sense of unity among orthodox Christians and gospel-celebrating churches.

Unity

The key to introducing anything new into a church's liturgy is patience and explanation. Don't rush the process of explanation and implementation. Allow ample opportunity to explain the value of a creed and to connect it to specific passages of Scripture. Jesus has tasked us with shepherding our people. We run the risk of shepherding with a heavy hand when we charge ahead and simply insist that we know best. Your church trusts you. Help them see that they have not misplaced their trust. Prioritize patient explanation of any change, especially a change in liturgy.

ACTION STEPS

1. Over the next 30 days, familiarize yourself with one creed, one confession, and one catechism.

2. Over the next 60 days, outline a plan for implementing the use of creeds, confessions, and catechisms in your church.

3. Over the next 90 days, begin introducing the creeds, confessions, and catechism to some of the key leaders within your church.

REFLECTION QUESTIONS

1. What are the function and purpose of creedal statements?

2. What is the difference between a creed and a confession?

3. How are creeds mandatory?

4. Why are confessions described as voluntary?

5. What are the three heresies mentioned in this chapter?

6. What are three benefits of corporate recitation of creeds?

RECOMMENDED READING

Tim Chester, *The Apostles' Creed* (Surrey, UK: The Good Book Company, 2006). Chester offers an accessible introduction to the value and biblical basis for the content of this historic creed.

Justin S. Holcomb, *Know the Creeds and Councils* (Grand Rapids: Zondervan, 2014). This small book is an excellent resource for studying the creeds personally or in a small group setting. I highly recommend this resource for action step 3.

J. I. Packer, *Affirming the Apostles' Creed* (Wheaton, IL: Crossway, 2008). Hospitable to both lay and learned audiences, J. I. Packer's work explains the theological implications contained within each line of the Apostles' Creed.

Carl R. Trueman, *The Creedal Imperative* (Wheaton, IL: Crossway, 2012). Trueman provides a clear and concise argument for why and how creeds and confessions should be used by evangelicals.

3

IMITATING CHRIST

One of the biggest regrets of my early Christian life is that I was never truly discipled, nor did I disciple anyone. While various men took an interest in me, there was no "follow me as I follow Christ" moment in any of our conversations, no rhythm of accountability and responsibility for one another. As a result, I studied in seminary largely as an island, and I entered ministry as an island. Talk about dangerous! The Christian life—let alone pastoral ministry—cannot be pursued in isolation. I remember realizing one day that I had spent most of my life in church, yet I had no idea what I was doing in living the Christian life.

How could this be? I never missed Sunday School or youth group, I attended Vacation Bible School every summer. I never missed a youth group summer camp trip. And I had my own flannel-graph board! What was wrong? Was it just me? How could I have spent so much time at church and church-related events but missed what it means to live the Christian faith? Sadly, most Christians I've known well have expressed the same thing.

Our efforts to make disciples systematically fail. We aren't discipling people. Instead we shuffle them through a checklist of activities and attendance records. Our churches are larger and richer than ever, but our biblical literacy, thirst for holiness, and spiritual discipline have never been poorer. Something has to change.

ANCIENT DEVOTION

The year before planting Redeemer Church, our launch team poured over the book of Acts. We weren't trying to replicate first-century Jerusalem. Instead, we wanted to understand what the first Christians valued and how those things influenced their daily lives. What I saw was something foreign to my own church experience. These Christians lived their lives together. In particular they devoted themselves to three things: the apostles' teaching, fellow believers, and Jesus' mission (Acts 2:42–47).

First, they devoted themselves to the apostles' teaching. What was the primary content of that teaching? The gospel. These first Christians were committed to the good news that the eternal Son of God had come in the flesh, lived the perfect and sinless life we cannot live, died the death we deserve on account of our sin, victoriously rose from the dead—defeating sin, death, and the devil—and ascended to the right hand of the Father, pouring out his Spirit on his people. Today, we have worn out the cliché of being "gospel centered." We've had to because so many churches are centered on anything and everything but the gospel. I imagine that the first Christians would find the phrase "gospel centered" humorous. After all, in their minds, what else could the church be?

Second, they devoted themselves to one another. They ate meals together. They worshiped together. They traveled together. They consistently spent time together in the intimacy of their homes. They prayed together—regularly and often. They met one another's physical needs, often at great personal expense. How radically different than many of our church experiences!

Third, they devoted themselves to the mission Jesus gave us. Living together and growing together in Scripture and the gospel, they made disciples. They invited their friends, neighbors, and co-workers into this community to meet Christians face to face and to hear firsthand what Christians believe. These unbelievers experienced a community of genuine love and Christlike self-sacrifice. The nature of this community was so powerful that new disciples were added daily.

In short, the early Christians wanted to be taught, they wanted to be known, and they wanted to proclaim Jesus. Based on this pattern, we planted Redeemer Church with three core values: gospel, community, and mission. We filter everything we do through these principles. Throughout the course of church history, you see these same values repeated again and again.

EARLY CHURCH DISCIPLESHIP—CHRISTIANS BUILD CHRISTIANS

Today, we have largely diminished "being a disciple" to making a profession of faith and receiving baptism. After that you're on your own. American rugged individualism has led us to act as if we do not need one another. The early church demanded more. The initial discipleship process for new converts included a regimented three-year plan for growing new believers in the grace and knowledge of Jesus.[1] New converts—called catechumens—regularly heard biblical preaching, received basic theological training, and renounced their sinful practices.[2]

Early Christians wrote a number of letters and tracts on discipleship. In his theological study on discipleship, titled *Following the Master*, Michael Wilkins demonstrates that the first Christians understood disciples to be those actively growing in the faith and consistently increasing in the knowledge of the gospel.[3] For example, Clement of Rome, who wrote near the end of the first century, refers to Christians as those who follow Jesus in the way of truth.[4] This should not take place in isolation, but in the community of Christ through mutual submission and meaningful relationships.[5] Polycarp's (69–155) exhortations in his *Epistle to the Philippians* are similar. He calls his readers to renounce sin, to pursue Christ, and to exemplify obedience in Christ.[6] *The Epistle to Diognetus* also reminded early Christians that disciples in Christ should consistently grow in truth and in the fruits of the Holy Spirit. While disciples must absolutely depend on God's Word and Spirit for this growth, they should also humbly listen to those who are more spiritually mature.[7] These early Christian authors recognized that we need one another. United to Christ, disciples grow together as Christ's members.

> ## Clement of Rome
>
> We know very little about this bishop other than his writings and brief references from Irenaeus (d. 202) and Tertullian (ca. 160–220), who mention him as the bishop of Rome during the last decade of the first century.

The rhythm practiced by the earliest Christians was one of relational mentoring.[8] Christians who were well-grounded in the faith would regularly engage with and teach those who were new to the faith. This practice built meaningful relationships, accountability, and responsibility into everyday Christian living. Moreover, it reminded believers of the need to grow in faith and theology.

PREACHERS BUILDING PREACHERS

One of the best things that ever happened to me in ministry was to be mentored by my senior pastor. As I gained experience in ministry, this pastor provided me with opportunities to preach and teach, he gave me helpful feedback, and he asked me about the state of my soul. This period of my life had a formative influence on the kind of pastor that I would become. Because of this experience, I now focus on intentionally training and encouraging future elders for our own congregation, as well as other churches.

I've learned a lot about mentoring from church history, particularly from Augustine and Charles Spurgeon. Augustine emphasized that mentoring requires an intense one-on-one relationship within the context of the community at large. Varied approaches—lecture, dialogue, and practical experience—are needed.[9] He focused especially on teachable believers who would in turn mentor others.[10] Even before his conversion, Augustine believed that the pursuit of truth necessitated the company of friends.[11] For him, the external exchange of ideas forges internal convictions. Thus, Augustine approached communal mentoring as an initiator and facilitator of extended conversations on matters of life, philosophy, and theology. These principles remain valuable for today.

Augustine (354–430)

Augustine's writings have profoundly shaped Western thought. His *Confessions* and *The City of God* are particularly influential.

Charles Spurgeon (1834–1892)

Dubbed "The Prince of Preachers," Spurgeon was England's best-known pastor during the 19th century.

Charles Spurgeon reflected a similar approach in his pastors college. This atypical educational institution focused on developing students at their own pace. Such an approach required intimate and specific knowledge of each student's intellectual capabilities based on personal interaction. Spurgeon approached ministerial preparation not in an industrialized fashion (that is, quantity over quality), but instead in the context of meaningful and vulnerable relationships. In this forum, Spurgeon instructed preachers in the art of preaching and the daily duties of pastoral ministry. To equip his students for ministry, Spurgeon spoke openly about the joys and struggles of the pastorate. By approaching education this way, rather than inculcating some abstract theory, he invited future pastors to imitate his life and ministry.[12]

Augustine and Spurgeon wanted to train pastors whose lives and faith their congregations would emulate. If pastors never invite others to follow them as they follow Jesus, who will? Churches need to see their pastors investing time and effort in others. Often pastors may not see the results of this faithful ministry, but future generations will. These disciples will be the next generation of church planters, elders, and missionaries. They in turn will disciple the church leaders of the future.

In the life of our church, we try to replicate the wisdom of Augustine and Spurgeon in training our leaders. For example, we have established a partnership with Southeastern Baptist Theological Seminary to provide seminary students with experience ministering in the local church. We prepare students for ministry through classroom lectures, practical experiences (e.g., overseeing one of our church's ministries), one-on-one and small group discipleship, and opportunities to preach. Our leadership team invites these students to imitate us as we imitate Christ (1 Cor 11:1). This call is central to the life of our church. Jesus asks that we be a people who are constantly investing in others.

PARENTS BUILDING CHILDREN

Catechizing children has long been important to disciple-making. Recognizing that this practice was standard in the early church, John Calvin exhorted all churches to reclaim this ancient practice. "How I wish that we might have kept the custom which ... existed among the ancient Christians!" he exclaimed concerning catechesis. Calvin saw catechesis as an opportunity for congregations to inculcate the one true faith, to help clarify and correct any misunderstandings among their youth. The benefits are great:

> If this discipline were in effect today, it would certainly arouse some slothful parents, who carelessly neglect the instruction of their children as a matter of no concern to them; for then they could not overlook it without public disgrace. There would be greater agreement in faith among Christian people, and not so many would go untaught and ignorant; some would not be so rashly carried away with new and strange doctrines; in short, all would have some methodical instruction, so to speak, in Christian doctrine.[13]

John Calvin

Based in Geneva, Calvin was one of the most important Protestant Reformers. His seminal work, *Institutes of the Christian Religion*, meant to be read with his commentaries, is one of the most influential theological works of the Reformation.

Puritans

These early English Protestants were ardently Reformed. They wanted to reform the English church according to "the regulative principle" (all worship practices must be explicitly sanctioned by Scripture), purging it of what they considered to be vestiges of Roman Catholicism. For example, they opposed the episcopal hierarchy, the use of vestments, and the uniform use of the Book of Common Prayer. Many Puritans fled to Holland and then to the New World to avoid religious persecution.

While some denominations have maintained this tradition, many have allowed its extinction. Baptists, for example, have rarely used catechisms in recent decades despite a heritage of children's catechisms since at least 1652. When we planted Redeemer Church, one of our goals was for parents and our congregation to work together to instruct children in the faith. For us, this meant parents participating in catechesis rather than relying on a professional children's ministry.

We strongly encourage children to participate in worship as soon as the parents believe they are mature enough. For those children who aren't ready, we offer a children's ministry heavily focused on making disciples. Each week, after a time of instruction, these children gather together to sing songs and hear a 15-minute version of the sermon, delivered by a staff member or intern. The children's sermon is full of illustrations that will connect with young audiences.

In addition, our staff and interns produce a weekly family discipleship guide for devotions and discipleship. These guides provide families with reflection questions from each week's sermon (which apply to children and adults), a memory verse from the sermon passage, catechism questions that reinforce the teaching of the passage, and suggestions for family devotions. These suggestions include sections of the text (from the previous Sunday's sermon) that could be discussed during the week, along with resources for younger children like *The Jesus Storybook Bible*.[14] For some, this approach to family worship and discipleship seems revolutionary. Many are surprised to learn that we have recontextualized an old practice mastered by the Puritans.[15]

WAYS TO RECLAIM IMITATION

First, begin with children.

All Christian parents want their children to know Scripture and to have a basic theological framework. Help them with this goal by introducing catechism questions into your children's ministry. Develop family discipleship guides that model the practice of catechizing children.

Second, introduce a catechism question for the month for small groups, adult Bible studies, or Sunday School classes.

Each month encourage the leaders of these groups to begin their time together with the question or series of questions. This is a good environment for introducing the parents in these groups to catechesis. This first step will create a sense of familiarity and comfort for that group and prepare them for introducing their own catechism questions at home.

Third, recapture the wonder of a gospel community.

No matter your church's existing discipleship structure, encourage one-on-one and small group discipleship. Our church uses sermon-based, in-home small groups to develop close relationships among believers and to grow them in their knowledge of Scripture. Each week, a series of discussion questions based on the sermon are prepared for our small group leaders. This kind of group gathering naturally lends itself to healthy discipleship habits (for example, confession of sin, Bible reading, prayer, etc.). If your church structure is not conducive to a large-scale launch of sermon-based small groups, perhaps you could offer weekly sermon-based discussion questions for small groups.

Fourth, invest in someone.

If pastors are not discipling someone, no one in their churches will either. One of the best things you can do for your church is to mentor someone. You will be surprised at the difference a discipling pastor makes in the life of a church. Begin building up future church planters, elders, and missionaries. Preparing Christians for ministry will renew your congregation's sense of the need to look outward rather than looking to meet their own needs. When a church embraces serving the global body of Christ by equipping and sending believers into their everyday mission fields, we truly gain a vision for fulfilling the Great Commission.

DEAR PASTOR,

For the church to maintain (or reclaim) a robust gospel witness in a culture increasingly indifferent to Christianity, you must grab hold of an aggressive and intentional plan for making disciples. When you look to the heroes of the past, you'll see that they intentionally invested in the lives of those around them. Conferences, while helpful, do not change people's lives. Instead, most stories of radical transformation or illumination involve rather routine but intentional conversations that reflect healthy patterns of discipleship. Those kinds of exchanges never happen if you live your life and carry out your ministry as an island.

ACTION STEPS

1. Identify two or three ways in which you can begin modeling the importance of discipleship for your church body.

2. Assess your personal discipleship habits. Identify those whom you are regularly discipling, irregularly discipling, and those whom you are building up for ministry.

3. After compiling this list, begin prioritizing your calendar around preaching the Word and discipling your congregation. Give priority to the leaders in your congregation and those whom you are preparing for ministry.

4. How could you partner with the nearest seminary or Bible college to prepare students for pastoral ministry? Find out what kinds of partnerships are available. Also, note the areas of opportunity in your church for seminary students to serve and gain experience.

5. In conjunction with a seminary or Bible college, develop a leadership pipeline where future pastors can gain experience, be discipled (by you), and then be launched for ministry.

REFLECTION QUESTIONS

1. What were the three commitments of the first Christians?

2. How did early Christians understand discipleship?

3. What are the benefits of catechesis?

4. How are you investing in your congregants?

5. How did Augustine and Charles Spurgeon support future pastors?

6. What is your church's plan and vision for raising up and sending out future pastors?

7. Why is it important for pastors to model discipleship habits for the church?

RECOMMENDED READING

Tim Chester and Steve Timmis, *Total Church: A Radical Reshaping around Gospel and Community* (Wheaton, IL: Crossway, 2008). This book has deeply influenced me. Chester and Timmis challenge everything they once thought was "church life." While not specifically on the subject of discipleship, *Total Church* helps readers begin to rethink what it means to acknowledge that Jesus is Lord over every aspect of their lives.

Paul R. House, *Bonhoeffer's Seminary Vision: A Case for Costly Discipleship and Life Together* (Wheaton, IL: Crossway, 2015). House demonstrates Bonhoeffer's commitment to theological education integrated into the ministry of the local church. This resource encourages pastors to develop an intentional model of ministry preparation and seminary students to pursue it.

Edward L. Smither, *Augustine as Mentor: A Model for Preparing Spiritual Leaders* (Nashville: B&H Academic, 2008). This is an excellent resource on discipleship practices. Smither models disciple-making in the local church through Augustine's methods, challenging pastors to mentor a group of congregants.

Jeff Vanderstelt, *Saturate: Being Disciples of Jesus in the Everyday Stuff of Life* (Wheaton, IL: Crossway, 2015). Vanderstelt wants to help Christians see that worship and discipleship are inseparable from Christians' lives. In this book Vanderstelt focuses on why discipleship matters more than explaining how to disciple. This is a great resource for the soul of a pastor.

4

PREACHING AND THE
CULTURAL DRIFT

I love teaching college and seminary courses. Most often, I find myself in settings that are warm and welcoming to my theology, my jokes about bad theology, and my Spurgeonesque assertion that all men should have beards. The first time I taught a college course in a secular setting, I was amused by how befuddled my students were that I am a pastor. I walked into class sporting a fauxhawk and skinny jeans. As I introduced myself, the students seemed encouraged by the thought of having a young professor that dressed and spoke as they do. I shared a brief overview of my academic background and showed a picture of my family. After a few snarky references to a recently released movie, I was accepted and welcomed. Then I shared what I do for a living. "I'm a pastor." The wind rushed out of the room. I mean, aren't all pastors old, racist homophobes who abhor pop culture and speak like their first cousin is Forrest Gump?

I was reminded how evangelicals are perceived: backwoods, irrelevant, and going the way of the dinosaur. By creating our own subcultures (and poor ones at that), we have lost our voice in the prevailing culture. We have not followed in the footsteps of our forebears in faith; instead we have largely retreated from society. The fallout from this retreat seems shocking, but it isn't.

Recent research reveals that roughly half of Millennials consider Scripture the Word of God in some sense—only half of that group believes all of Scripture to be the Word of God.[1] The church's scriptural message is increasingly foreign to those around us. How have we responded? Have we even noticed? We may very well provide more hindrances than helps! These findings reflect the observation of the cultural apologetic scholar William Edgar: "Christians have grown so used to their own language, terms, and culture that they have become isolated from those who surround them."[2]

There are two parts to the problem. First, we have falsely assumed in our proclamation that our listeners share our Christian worldview. Second, because we're failing to address the presuppositions of their worldview, our audience isn't even listening.

John Broadus (1827–1895)

John Broadus served as the Southern Baptist Theological Seminary's New Testament professor and second president. Charles Spurgeon once referred to this respected expositor as "the greatest of living preachers."

Too often our preaching has been like our view of history: dead and lifeless. Had evangelicals not abandoned the wisdom of our forebears, we would have maintained a much more persuasive and public witness in America. One of the greatest preachers in my tradition, John Broadus (1827–1895), wrote of the value of church history to preaching and teaching Scripture:

> Church History does not usually receive from working ministers the attention it deserves. Especially does the history of Doctrines assist one in understanding the truth, and in comprehending those objections and erroneous tendencies, which under different forms reproduce themselves in every age.[3]

Broadus exhorts us to consider the value of church history for preparing and delivering a sermon. In his estimation, many errors could be avoided, and many falsehoods corrected, if pastors were more familiar with church history and historical theology.

Now, as American culture becomes increasingly indifferent to Christian messages and mores, we must learn from the example of past Christians. Christian leaders have always accommodated their message to their audience, while carefully articulating Christian doctrine and its logical outcomes.

LOUD NOISES!

When I first arrived in India, I regularly encountered people who could not understand me. I would unconsciously repeat myself loudly and slowly. As soon as I became aware of what I was doing, I was embarrassed for being the ugly American. Much of our preaching and even more of the evangelical outreach to the cultures around us have mirrored this linguistic disconnect. If we could just be loud enough, our neighbors will understand us! However, we see that many effective pastors throughout church history took a far different approach to engaging their listeners.

To be sure, there have always been those who decried the use of philosophy, pagan culture, and contextualization in explaining Scripture. For instance, Tertullian (ca. 160–230) famously wrote, "What indeed has Athens to do with Jerusalem?"[4] His point was that we cannot allow the prevailing philosophical commitments of our day to drive our theological agenda. Undoubtedly, Tertullian's warning has merit; Scripture must always dictate the content of our preaching. However, Tertullian's legacy is his contribution to Trinitarian theology—and he repurposed the popular jargon of the day and pre-existing philosophical concepts to do so.[5] We cannot totally escape from context, no matter how hard we

Tertullian (ca. 160–230)

Tertullian was the first theologian to refer to the Godhead as "the Trinity." He wrote robust defenses of the oneness of God while maintaining the distinctions among the persons of the Godhead. He is also known for his five-volume response to Marcion, an influential second-century heretic.

try. We must engage the worldview presuppositions of our context to more clearly communicate Christian doctrine. Neither theology nor preaching occurs in a vacuum.

Augustine of Hippo wrote one of the first textbooks for young preachers. This influential theologian communicated skillfully; he masterfully employed analogies and illustrations. Augustine encouraged his students to study famous pagan orators to learn effective communication styles and language patterns.[6] Augustine did not intend for his students to minimize Scripture or to dismiss its claims—that is, he didn't mean that pastors should merely be sanctified Jim Gaffigans or Jon Stewarts—but that they should communicate in a manner that was understandable to their audience.

Augustine's suggestion reflects what the first church historian, Luke, observed. In the Acts of the Apostles, Luke records that the Apostle Paul made use of his listeners' context. In Acts 14, while speaking to a largely agrarian audience, Paul makes frequent reference to agrarian terminology. Paul and Barnabas insisted that the God they worshiped is the very God who made the land, sea, and the creatures that dwell there. Further, the Creator is the one who controls the changing of the seasons, the provision of rain, and the abundance of crops (Acts 14:14–18). Most famously, in Acts 17, Paul appeals to pagan philosophy and theology as he bridges the cultural divide between him and his audience. He made use of the people's pre-existing philosophical and theological categories to direct their attention to the God of Scripture. Paul immersed himself in the milieu in which his audience lived and thought, and he used their worldview presuppositions to present the gospel more convincingly.

During the Reformation, Luther became the standard-bearer for the power and clarity of Protestant preaching. Luther was known for his bluntness, accessibility, and linguistic relevance in the pulpit. Luther directly interacted with his culture: He used familiar language and illustrations. When some challenged his colloquial translations as unfaithful to the very words of Scripture, he vigorously defended his approach.

What is the point of needlessly adhering so stiffly and stubbornly to the words, so that we can't understand it at all? Whoever wants to speak German must not use Hebrew style. Rather he must see to it—once he understands the Hebrew author—that he concentrates on the sense of the text and thinks, 'Dear man, how do Germans speak in such a situation?' Once he has the German words to serve the purpose, let him drop the Hebrew words and express the meaning freely in the best German he knows.[7]

For Luther, the substance of Scripture dictates how we translate it. He insisted that Scripture be understandable to the unlearned; he regularly reminded his peers that preachers must accommodate the gospel message to children and servants, not educated theologians and humanists.[8]

In the 20th century, Francis Schaeffer arose as a mix of Aristotle, Jonathan Edwards, and Grizzly Adams; he dedicated himself to theology, philosophy, and art. Schaeffer routinely warned of the moral decline facing America. He also called for Christians to learn history and engage culture in a straightforward and germane fashion. In *Escape from Reason* he states, "Each generation of the church in each setting has the responsibility of communicating the gospel in understandable terms, considering the language and thought-forms of that setting."[9] We must take this call seriously. We must recognize the divide between our Christian worldview and the prevailing worldview of our society, and we must work hard to overcome this barrier to fulfill the Great Commission in our context.

RECOVERING APOLOGETICS

In their early sermons, the apostles proclaimed the Lord Jesus, who he is and what he has done and will do. To do this, the apostles often had to defend against misinterpretation of these truths. In Acts 2, Peter preaches the gospel message by explaining Scripture, and defends these claims by referencing the miracles of Jesus. In Acts 17, Paul reasons with the Athenians through preaching the resurrection of Jesus and using philosophical language that his listeners understand. In the very next chapter, Apollos preaches about the ministry of Jesus and refutes those who would deny that Jesus is the Messiah.

Beyond the sermons preached by the first Christians, much of Scripture itself is written with an eye toward apologetic implications. The first chapters of Genesis are both a scriptural account of creation and an apologetic against ancient Near Eastern cosmogonies. Even many of the miracles recorded in Scripture are meant to serve apologetic purposes. These miracles range from the plagues in Egypt, demonstrating the futility of Egyptian gods, to the healing miracles performed by Jesus, revealing that he is the Messiah. The text of Scripture is so interwoven with apologetic elements that it is difficult to preach the whole counsel of God without noting those elements and incorporating them into weekly sermons.

Apologetics

The branch of Christian theology that seeks to defend the truth claims of the Christian faith.

The first preachers of Scripture recognized the need for rational argumentation, culturally relevant appeals to logic and reason, and apologetics. In an increasingly hostile culture, this kind of proclamation becomes ever more important. For example, we are not the first generation of Christians to wrestle with complicated sexual issues. In his *Second Apology*, Justin Martyr discusses issues related to a former life of sexual sin. The sins that Justin addresses were widely accepted in that society. Justin carefully but directly engages not only what the gospel has to say about these sins, but also the public fallout from the church's repudiation of the larger culture's accepted behavior.[10] Centuries later, his words are of great value as the sexual revolution marches on in the United States and raises serious questions regarding what can be considered hate-speech in future years. Many have navigated similar terrain before us; their example can encourage and instruct us.

> ## Justin Martyr
>
> One of the first Christian philosophers, Justin used the Apostle John's *logos* language to explain the deity of Jesus to his audience. He was also one of the first to publicly defend the Christian right to worship.

WHY CONTEXTUALIZATION AND APOLOGETICS IN PREACHING?

Preaching requires enculturation and apologetics. For example, in an age of increasing skepticism and ever-present access to materials from people like Bart Ehrman, it is often helpful to provide basic apologetic arguments at the onset of every new book or sermon series. Sometimes I defend Pauline authorship of letters like 2 Timothy. I do this because the work of people like Ehrman has influenced many to believe that we have no idea who wrote the books of the Bible. While the authorship of some texts is unknown, Scripture is hardly anonymous; the source of all Scripture is God himself (2 Tim 3:16). Other times I address hot-button issues such as whether Scripture condones chattel slavery. Due to the claims of reductionistic but catchy memes and opinion pieces on Old Testament laws, I must clarify what Scripture says about human dignity and the value of life.

Some texts of Scripture easily lend themselves to apologetic application (such as 1 Cor 15), while others are more difficult (for example, Song of Songs). Yet in today's culture, the presentation of even the most innocuous of passages would benefit from an apologetic. For instance, when speaking of the gospel picture implicit within the relationship between a husband and wife (Eph 5:31–33), we must preach (even briefly) an apologetic for God's definition of marriage. The marriage covenant is one of the clearest pictures of the gospel (a husband seeks and serves his bride as Christ seeks and serves his Church), and it has practical applications for Christian living. So, we cannot ignore giving an apologetic for the scriptural understanding of marriage.

Go Deeper: Apologetics

Ancient Christian Texts, eds. Thomas C. Oden and Gerald L. Bray (Downers Grove, IL: IVP Academic, 2009-).

Ancient Christian Commentary on Scripture, 29 vols., ed. Thomas C. Oden (Downers Grove, IL: InterVarsity Press, 1998-2009).

Reformation Commentary on Scripture, 28 vols. projected, eds. Timothy George and Scott M. Manetsch (Downers Grove, IL: IVP Academic, 2011-).

Apologetics may seem to fall outside the context of corporate worship, since many consider it part of personal evangelism. However, when the church gathers to worship through Word and song, this time is for the instruction and edification of the saints. We cannot expect that congregants are not influenced by our culture or that they do not battle with doubt. When the people of God gather together, they do so to have their confidence in God's Word confirmed and strengthened. Moreover, regardless of whether we recognize it, most Christians adopt their pastor's interpretation and application of Scripture as their own. Therefore, if we model an apologetic-free approach to the biblical text, that is what our people will practice. If pastors assume that their listeners know the foundation of a Christian truth claim, like Christ's deity, their congregations never see those claims unpacked so that they, too, can defend them and build on them. We should not assume that our congregation is in agreement with whatever scriptural propositional claim we are addressing. Thus, in an effort to edify and build up the body of Christ, we must "contend earnestly for the faith" (Jude 3) from the pulpit so that the pew will be a place of confidence and a place of preparation for cultural engagement.

RELEVANTLY RELEVANT AND LOGICALLY LOGICAL

I have a very basic pattern for engaging worldview issues in teaching and preaching. Regardless of the worldview concept being addressed, I ask the following questions:

First, how is this issue portrayed or explored in pop culture?

Most Americans develop their worldview through the public school system and pop culture. Schaeffer masterfully assessed the worldview promoted and presented in various forms of art. By engaging the underlying worldview presuppositions of art, he helped shape an entire generation of Christians. Following Schaeffer's pattern, I try to uncover the implicit worldview of a given art form or expression of pop culture. What is it teaching? What are its long-term implications?

Second, what are the socio-political ramifications for this topic?

Same-sex marriage was discussed in movies, music, video games, and sitcoms long before it became the political cause of the day. Recognizing and even addressing (in a fair and kind posture) the sociopolitical implications of current worldview discussions is incredibly advantageous. The members of your congregation are digesting the content of the worldview around them. If we do not proactively equip our congregants to think biblically on trending issues, they may passively adopt the unbiblical positions propagated around them. Justin Martyr tried to do this by stating how Christian values benefit all people. We must reflect his example.

Third, how can I faithfully and scripturally address this issue in simple and contemporary language?

The model of Christians like Augustine and Luther shows us how to hold to a robust theology while speaking in a winsome fashion. The answer to this question will provide you with the content and tools necessary to address difficult issues with brevity and clarity. For instance, I was once invited to participate in a sexual ethics panel discussion at a secular college. Just as the panel was concluding, the moderator asked me—the only evangelical on the panel—to explain why God wouldn't want everyone to be happy by freeing them to explore their sexuality to its fullest expression. I had 60 seconds to respond. Thankfully, I had already considered this question. I referenced "That '70s Show" as a culturally relevant illustration that created a bridge to God's purpose and design for human sexuality as described in Scripture. We must be prepared for opportunities like these.

These days, I spend less time in secular classrooms. However, as I have reflected on my interactions with those students, I have recognized a pattern. Each semester began and ended in the same way. The initial shock that a normal, educated, culturally relevant, evangelical exists eventually wore off. Throughout each semester we exchanged ideas, discussed serious worldview issues, quoted random movie lines, and engaged in real relationships that replaced stereotypes. Although some of my students eventually came to saving faith in Jesus, the majority remained in unbelief. However, my attempts to provide rational reasons for my faith, and the culturally relevant manner in which I communicated those reasons, bridged the communication gap between my students and me. Still, no matter how much we attempt to integrate widely known references or logical argumentation into our preaching and teaching, the work of conversion always belongs to the Holy Spirit. Even so, the regular means by which the Spirit changes hearts and minds is gospel preaching by gospel people.

DEAR PASTOR,

You must exegete culture, relying on the guidance of the Spirit and the authority of Scripture, as you seek to faithfully preach the gospel to the world around you.

ACTION STEPS

1. Dedicate 30 minutes a day, for 30 days, to observing how Christians are described in the news, on social media platforms, and in influential publications.

2. Note how certain elements of the Christian worldview and Christian vocabulary are lost on those commenting on Christianity.

3. Remove vague Christian language from your vocabulary. Ask those around you to point out some of your usual Christianisms.

4. Define, at least briefly, basic Christian concepts and words.

5. Over the course of a year, slowly transition your preaching style and language toward an approach that reflects commitment to the biblical text and an understanding of the culture.

REFLECTION QUESTIONS

1. What is the two-fold problem in Christian proclamation?

2. What can studying the history of Christian doctrine help preachers avoid?

3. Why did some early church theologians object to the use of pagan language in preaching?

4. Who was the first theologian to use "Trinity" to describe the Godhead?

5. Which influential church father encouraged his students to use the communication styles of prominent pagan orators while expositing Scripture?

6. What are the three questions we should ask as we engage worldview issues in our preaching?

RECOMMENDED READING

John Broadus, *A Treatise on the Preparation and Delivery of Sermons* (Louisville, KY: The Southern Baptist Theological Seminary, 2012). This is one of the most influential books on preaching within my tradition. The value of this book is in its approach to the method of sermon research and writing.

Timothy Keller, *Preaching: Communicating Faith in an Age of Skepticism* (New York: Viking Press, 2015). Keller is a master of biblical exposition and thoughtful cultural engagement. This book is less a manual for delivering a sermon and more of a exhortation to good public speaking. Still, Keller's ability to engage any audience is a skill that all pastors must learn to develop. This text will prove most helpful in this endeavor.

Tony Merida, *Faithful Preaching: Declaring Scripture with Responsibility, Passion, and Authority* (Nashville: B&H Academic, 2009). Merida has profoundly influenced my approach to preaching. This book is one of the most accessible and useful texts on preaching. Merida models faithful exposition and cultural engagement in a way that few authors are able to do.

Charles Spurgeon, *Lectures to My Students* (Peabody, MA: Hendrickson, 2010). A classic work that represents Charles Spurgeon's understanding of both preaching and preparation to preach (along with various pastoral duties). While not focused solely on preaching, Spurgeon's comments are helpful.

5

CHRISTIANS AND CULTURE

I had a brief stint as the manager of a Christian bookstore. One day, as I spoke with a customer about our music selection (while comparing Christian artists to their secular counterparts), it dawned on me that much of what we were selling wasn't good. The issue was the derivative quality of the content. Many artists weren't focused on creating good music; instead they emulated the style of a certain secular artist.

The rest of the day, I caught myself making statements like, "If you like Youtube, you will love Godtube," or, "If you like Stephen King, then you will feel right at home reading Frank Peretti's latest novel." The difficult truth I had come to accept was that Christians spend far too much time consuming secular culture or cheap Christian subcultures instead of producing good culture. To make matters worse, this epiphany came as I wore "A bread crumb & Fish" shirt, a laughably bad knock-off of Abercrombie & Fitch. Rather than creating art or music grounded in our identity as Christ's members, we too often try to pull a bait and switch. We parrot the culture around us. We look like they do and sound

Culture

Bruce Ashford gives one of the most succinct and uniquely Christian definitions of culture: "Culture is anything humans produce when they interact with each other and God's creation."

like they do, but we claim there's something about us that makes everything different: Jesus. But where's the difference?

As I entered into pastoral ministry, I continued this habit. It wasn't good. I began to wonder how we could preach a gospel that redeems the world while failing to produce good culture. Christians seem to approach culture in one of two ways: to hide from the prevailing culture or to crank out rip-offs of the prevailing culture (often slapping a Jesus fish on it). Reflecting on whether there's a better way, I realized that our ceaseless production of culture—books, paintings, and songs—droned on without intentionality. In journeying through church history, I began to see that the first Christians were not subcultural; they were countercultural. Their culture was not derivative, but truly creative. They produced good culture that influenced the larger culture.

The first Christians did not abandon cultural engagement. However, upon coming to faith in Jesus, they viewed themselves as citizens of another kingdom with allegiance to another king. The Christian claim that "Jesus is Lord" struck at the heart of Roman identity. Romans believed that the health of their society—politically and economically—depended heavily on reverencing and appeasing the Roman pantheon.[1] As result, when calamity visited a city or region with a large Christian population, many blamed the Christians. Nevertheless, the first believers continued to consider themselves an outpost of this otherworldly kingdom that would one day replace every kingdom of the world. By producing good culture that reflected a respect for human dignity, care for the poor, and reverence for God, these Christians were countercultural and culturally creative people.

The City of God

Augustine wrote this book in response to the popular charge that Christians caused the decline of the Roman Empire.

Today's secular culture is greatly influenced by an early Christian's book: *The City of God*. In it Augustine addresses the principal Roman understanding of politics, philosophy, theology, and culture. He praises what is good and in accordance with Scripture. For instance, he highlights Plato's three-fold division of philosophy as reflecting God's truth.[2] He also criticizes the predominant culture and art forms of the day. He argues, for example, that Rome has endured because of God's will, not because of the Roman pantheon.[3] Indeed, the Roman devotion to the gods resulted in a faulty, even wicked morality, expressed through art forms like theater.[4] Finally, Augustine explains God's final judgment by comparing the worldly city with the heavenly city. Even so, *The City of God* is one of the foundational pillars for an increasingly worldly Western culture.[5]

Abraham Kuyper (1837–1920), one of the most influential Christian theologians, reinvigorated the notion that we ought to redeem culture and produce culture. Kuyper drew heavily on Calvin's insistence that Jesus is sovereign over all things and that the entire world is the theater of God. He did this as a pastor, who led his church and his nation as a culture-maker. Kuyper insisted that believers ought to seek the good of those around them by living out the values of a distinctly Christian culture in every vocation of life. Being a Christian is not somehow incidental to who we are; it is essential. We must view everything we produce, build, and create through our identity as followers of Christ. Only then can we properly redeem and produce culture.

> ## Abraham Kuyper (1837–1920)
>
> The son of a pastor and a pastor himself, Kuyper founded the Amsterdam Free University, served multiple terms in parliament, and spent four years as the Prime Minister of the Netherlands (1901–1905).

Kuyper sought to generate good culture through writing books, through political action, and through educating Christians. In his estimation of Kuyper's impact, Bruce Ashford highlights how we can follow in Kuyper's example: We may not found a university, "but we can shape our children's education toward Christ"; we may never run for president, "but we can vote and interact politically in a way that honors

Christ."[6] Kuyper believed that the church, specifically pastors, ought to lead in producing positive, persuasive, Christ-honoring culture that benefits society as a whole. Scripture tells us that God ordained human beings to exercise dominion over all creation (Gen 1:26). Human beings are to mirror their Creator, who brought order from chaos (Gen 1:2). For Kuyper, this mandate necessitates education that reflects a Christian worldview and political action grounded in biblical ethics. Many Christians in the West have ignored this mandate.

Today, many pastors wrestle with balancing the rejection of anti-Christian culture and the production of good Christian culture. After the fundamentalist controversies in the late-19th and early 20th centuries, pastors (and Christians in general) tend to react to the prevailing cultural norms of the day. For instance, shortly after American universities embraced Darwinian evolution, some pastors like Henry Ward Beecher (1813-1887) thought that cultural reform must be joined to a pared-down version of Christianity. He advocated a mutual conditioning of gospel culture and modern culture. While Beecher believed that social reform was necessary to usher in the kingdom of God on earth, he was also convinced that for the church to survive in the modern world, certain doctrines ought to be abandoned or accommodated to the latest scientific and philosophical claims.[7] Beecher's ideas regarding the authority of Scripture, social progress, and the kingdom of God became normative among theologically liberal pastors and denominations.

Henry Ward Beecher (1813–1887)

The brother of Harriet Beecher Stowe, Henry became known as a politically minded pastor who favored a liberal reading of Scripture. He was lauded for his advocacy of the abolitionist movement. He was eventually put on trial under the charge of adultery.

At the same time, many theologically conservative Christians filtered cultural interaction through a new theological system called dispensationalism. For these people, holding to the fundamentals of the Christian faith meant holding to a pessimistic view of history, cities, and culture as a whole.[8] This shift was in stark contrast to the postmillennial hope that permeated American Christianity before the American Revolution. Largely popularized by influential people like D. L. Moody (1837–1899), this new pessimism was employed as an evangelistic tool. Moody preached that the continued moral decline of all cultures was inevitable. Thus, to be faithful to Christ meant to retreat from the world. While effective in calling many to repentance, this approach also called Christians out of the culture and into churches that functioned as bunkers rather than those issuing a call for a better culture under the rule of a better King.

Dispensationalism

John Nelson Darby (1800–1882) crafted this premillennial system of biblical interpretation that assumes God's plan for humanity unfolds differently through different and distinct dispensations of time.

Postmillennialism

This optimistic eschatology teaches that Christ's reign is ushered in by the successful preaching of the gospel. Leading up to Christ's second coming, things will get better not worse. Not all postmillennialists affirm a literal 1000-year millennium. Jonathan Edwards (1703–1758) was a prominent early American postmillennialist.

D. L. Moody (1837–1899)

With only a fifth-grade education, Moody founded Moody Bible Institute and popularized the Sunday school movement. Moody was one of the most renowned evangelists in American history. Some estimate that he preached to more than 100 million people.

The sad result of retreat and antagonism is that the prevailing culture has begun its collapse into moral anarchy. Without significant Christian voices and cultural influences, a vacuum has formed, and there is no suitable, satisfying cultural norm that can fill the void. In its search for beauty, the prevailing culture has destroyed beauty by celebrating pornographic consumption. In its search for meaningful artistic expression, secular culture has venerated nihilistic imagery that denigrates the Creator and the creature. What ought to terrify us is this inevitable truth: Any nation that embraces a culture of death will find, in its end, the death of culture.

THE CULTURE-MAKING IMPERATIVE

Evangelicals in the West seem to have failed to engage, reform, and create culture. Schaeffer predicted that the results will be disastrous. The pursuit of personal peace and prosperity, unchecked by the Christian love of God and neighbor, will lead to economic woes, increased violence, terrorist actions, threats to natural resources and the environment, and eventually the insistence that all people submit to the moral values of the dominant culture.[9] While the church may seem to have been in the bunkers for far too long, we are always only one generation away from a new cultural collapse or cultural reformation.

After describing this grim future for the church, Schaeffer encourages us that "as Christians we are not only to know the right worldview, the worldview that tells us the truth of what is, but consciously to act upon that worldview so as to influence society in all its parts and facets across the whole spectrum of life, as much as we can to the extent of our individual and collective ability."[10]

THE WAY FORWARD

Throughout history, the most culturally influential Christians have been pastors: Augustine, John Calvin, Martin Luther, Abraham Kuyper, and Francis Schaeffer. Pastors are critical for progress in redeeming and producing culture. We must understand the culture around us, help build redemptive culture, and envision how to create culture.

Pastors must be cultural exegetes.

It is our duty to understand the culture and its values. It amazes me that we recognize this responsibility for missionaries, but we fail to emphasize this in the ministry of a pastor. Missionaries are trained and expected to grow in their understanding of the society in which they are ministering. We send out missionaries, knowing that they will dedicate much of their time to learning a foreign culture and language. In many ways, the culture in which Christians find themselves is both familiar and foreign. Like Augustine, we pastors must learn, explain, and respond to the prevailing culture in order to cast a vision for reforming it.

Pastors must be culture makers.

A century ago, pastors were recognized writers, artists, and societal experts. When someone wanted to understand a particular political philosophy or the underlying message of a specific piece of artwork, they knew they could look to their pastor. Pastors both exegeted the culture and intentionally led in producing culture. Today, we are increasingly relegated to characterizations that make it seem as if all of us—believers and especially pastors—are on equal footing with Boss Hogg from the Dukes of Hazard. Change this perception by changing your actions. Read widely and deeply, write clearly, and speak with educated authority on matters pertaining to culture.

Pastors must be cultural visionaries.

Present a compelling vision to your congregation for why Christians must produce Christian art. You must encourage your congregants to use their God-given artistic talents to produce culture—painting, photography, music, writing, and social media—that reflects a biblical worldview. For decades, the church has failed to encourage artistic expression. The result has been that many of the thoughtful expressions of artistry in our society have reflected an unbiblical worldview. This doesn't mean that we only paint pictures of biblical stories, or that we only make movies about some kind of emotional conversion to faith in Jesus. Instead, we must produce good art because our biblical worldview uniquely allows us to celebrate beauty. Further, we can demonstrate our ability for meaningful, uplifting, artistic expression grounded in the fact that we are created in the image of an artistic God. Because we bear the image of God, we naturally desire to reflect (in a finite way) his artistry.

DEAR PASTOR,

Tasked with shepherding souls under the leadership of the Good Shepherd, you must make a choice. You can continue your life as Mr. Magoo, happily ignorant and unengaged with the world around you as you perpetuate our derivative Christian subcultures, or you can respond to the charge given to you by the history of the church. Will you retreat and hide from culture, or will you be a culture-maker like Augustine, Kuyper, and Schaeffer? You have a great task before you, but you are not alone. Many have come before you, and they have left examples for you to follow. So, put away your "A bread crumb & Fish" shirt and delete your Godtube account. Speak into the culture and make culture.

ACTION STEPS

1. Create a list of cultural expressions that can be readily found within your context (city, neighborhood, etc.).

2. Discern how Christians are either intentionally engaging or disengaging from these expressions of culture.

3. Develop a roadmap, for yourself and your church, as to how Christians could better engage the culture within your context.

4. Cast a vision for producing good culture in your church body. Supply your church with at least three examples for how Christians have historically produced meaningful culture.

REFLECTION QUESTIONS

1. What is culture?

2. How did Abraham Kuyper create culture?

3. What is cultural exegesis?

4. How can you be a culture maker?

5. What does it mean to be a cultural visionary?

RECOMMENDED READING

Bruce Riley Ashford, *Every Square Inch: An Introduction to Cultural Engagement for Christians* (Bellingham, WA: Lexham Press, 2015). This is one of the best introductions to cultural engagement—how you can begin to understand, engage, and produce culture. Ashford also does an excellent job of referring the reader to historical resources and examples.

Andy Crouch, *Culture Making: Recovering Our Creative Calling* (Downers Grove, IL: InterVarsity Press, 2009). Providing a holistic definition of culture, Crouch overviews how churches have historically responded to the prevailing culture, and he casts a vision for ways believers should intentionally create culture.

Colin Duriez, *Francis Schaeffer: An Authentic Life* (Wheaton, IL: Crossway, 2008). This is my favorite biography of Schaeffer. It's an excellent resource for those interested in how Schaeffer engaged culture as a pastor.

Richard Mouw, *Abraham Kuyper: A Short and Personal Introduction* (Grand Rapids: Eerdmans, 2011). Mouw offers an easily accessible introduction to Kuyper's life, thought, and view of culture.

Francis A. Schaeffer, *How Should We Then Live?: The Rise and Decline of Western Thought and Culture* (Wheaton, IL: Crossway, 2005). One of Schaeffer's most influential works, this text provides a blueprint for cultural exegesis. I recommend reading this book with the accompanying video series.

6

YESTERDAY, TODAY

WAS THE FUTURE

I'm not sure what is more fully represented by Nicolas Cage starring in the *Left Behind* reboot: the demise of serious American filmmaking or the church's incessant obsession with the future. Christians are continually looking toward the future. We are obsessed with it. That's why the *Left Behind* book series has sold more than 63 million copies, and why disgraced televangelists can make successful comebacks by selling "apocalypse ready" food. And on account of this obsession with the future, groups like Barna Research and LifeWay Research work hard to translate current church trends into future projections, but these educated guesses aren't necessarily more accurate than anyone else's conjecture. We're so busy worrying about the future that we neglect to consider how the past might equip us for today and tomorrow. The future by its nature is unknowable. Still, we can prepare for what will come by looking to the past.

For example, as I write this final chapter, some are worried about the future of religious liberty in the United States, but the current trend is nothing that the church hasn't seen before. In fact, the American experience of relative peaceful coexistence between the church and state has largely been a historical anomaly. Church history has been dominated by struggle and strife. So how can the past help us negotiate the present and prepare for the future?

BE PREPARED

The past shows us that we have always been viewed as a subversive people who follow a subversive King.

Pontius Pilate's questioning of Jesus demonstrates that we have always been viewed through a lens of suspicion (John 18:28–40). The charges made against the first Christians further confirm that governments recognize the necessarily "rebellious" intent of professing Jesus is Lord. Our current unpopularity should not make us feel alone. Instead, American Christians join in the experience of popular disapproval that the Church has experienced for 2,000 years.

Looking to the past can help us recognize successful and unsuccessful methods for communicating the gospel in a hostile context. Whether we look to the contents of 1 Peter or read the writings of Justin Martyr, we must embrace the wisdom of those who have faithfully presented the good news in hostile contexts, long before our nation was even founded.

We can rest assured that gospel progress is never linear, but it is always typified by breakthroughs, failures, victories, and reforms. From the time of the apostles to today, the church has experienced numerous government-sanctioned persecutions, the rise and increase of heretics and Christian cults, and the implementation and removal of religious freedom. We have also seen doctrine clarified and recovered. Even when times seem difficult, the past shows us that Jesus keeps his promise that even the gates of hell would not prevail against his Church (Matt 16:17–19).

Knowing church history will enable you to love and lead the body of Christ well.

In shepherding the people with whom Christ has entrusted you, remember that you are tasked with leading them well. It is no easy task. Calvin describes it this way:

> Here, then, is the sovereign power with which the pastors of the church, by whatever name they be called, ought to be endowed. That is that they may dare boldly to do all things by God's Word;

may compel all worldly power, glory, wisdom, and exaltation to yield to and obey his majesty; supported by his power, may command all from the highest even to the last; may build up Christ's household and cast down Satan's; may feed the sheep and drive away the wolves; may instruct and exhort the teachable; may accuse, rebuke, and subdue the rebellious and stubborn; may bind and loose; finally, if need be, may launch thunderbolts and lightnings; but do all things in God's Word.[1]

You would be foolish to attempt to preach doctrine that is not in accord with historic orthodoxy, but how can you know historic orthodoxy without knowing history? It is madness to lament the failure of your church to produce healthy disciples, unless you are willing to explore and to use the practices and methods of discipleship that have yielded great success for nearly two millennia. It is stubborn foolishness to debate how to winsomely defend Christian truth claims without consulting the examples of biblically consistent and culturally relevant apologetic efforts from church history. It is a vain exercise to fret over the demise of the prevailing culture, unless you are willing to join with those in the past who sought to create good culture and to reform sub-biblical culture. Finally, it is a pitiful dereliction of your pastoral duties if you allow your church members to live in fear of what might come in the future, if you fail to remind them of what God has done in the past among his people.

Learn from others, including the giants.

I used to suffer from chronological snobbery, but that wasn't my only problem. I was also arrogant, rude, and condescending to those who were not enlightened enough to hold to my particular theology. I went so far as to change my "religious views" on my Facebook page to "correct." Moreover, I saw myself as a great gift to the church. This hubris came through in the tone of my sermons. I didn't love the Bride of Christ well. I was a ministry train wreck waiting to happen.

The more I studied church history, the more I realized that I was a theological bully. (Don't misunderstand me: There are doctrinal non-negotiables that we must defend, earnestly.) I was more concerned with conformity—as in conforming to what I believed—than I was with gospel unity in my church. As my understanding of church history grew, my pride was dismantled.

I realized that many of the secondary doctrines (for example, eschatological views)—ones I prided myself for believing—cost many of our forebears their lives. I wasn't extraordinary for believing these doctrines; instead, I was the beneficiary of extraordinary men and women. I learned that earnest, but strident Christians like Luther submitted themselves to the Word of God, desiring their thoughts, words, and deeds to be reproved, corrected, and built up in God's righteousness. Often this means admitting that you're wrong.

I saw how theological giants such as Augustine, Calvin, and Jonathan Edwards preached boldly, but with the tenderness of shepherds who cared for their sheep. They preached truth, not from a position of arrogance, but from a posture of humble submission to Scripture. Moreover, I recognized that those mentioned throughout this book never sought to be heroes of the faith. They pursued faithfulness. While I assumed that I was a gift to the church, those who impacted the Church for all ages were content with loving the Bride of Christ. I began to see a pattern emerging: Those who affected the Church the most were more concerned with the story of Christ's Bride, his Church, than their own story. In a moment of sobering thought, led by the Holy Spirit, I recognized that church history is the story of Christ's Bride growing, preparing, and being prepared for her wedding (Rev 19–20).

HOPE FOR ALL AGES

Throughout every era of Christian history, there have been high and low points. There have been heroes, heretics, and villains. Still, there has been one constant: hope. This hope is grounded in the good news. The one who sustains his people is the very one who lived the life we could not live, and died the death we deserve, to pay the debt we could not pay, and rose again to give us abundant life free from the slavery of sin and death. Having ascended to the Father, our Lord Jesus continues to keep his promise to never forsake his people by sending the Holy Spirit to indwell, empower, unite, and sanctify his people.

There is hope because Jesus purchased the Church by his blood, he sustains the Church by his Word and Spirit, and he is coming again for his Bride, the Church. No matter what the coming years have in store, the hope of the Church and the hope for you, dear pastor, has never changed: Jesus wins. Join with the echo that resounds from ages past: "He will come again, in glory, to judge the living and the dead; his kingdom will have no end."[2]

DEAR PASTOR,

Church history has changed my ministry and my life. Through it, as well as through Scripture and fellowship, the Spirit of Christ continues to shape me more into the image of Christ. The effects of studying church history are bountiful; the one for which I am most thankful is a growing sense of humility. I'm just a momentary blip in the grand story of the Church—the same Church that the King of heaven sought and bought with his own blood, and in his kindness and love he entrusts and empowers me to serve.

Pastor, one of the greatest gifts you can receive from the study of church history is humility. We are not giants; instead, we stand on the shoulders of giants. We are not writing our own story; we are part of the great story of redemption in which Christ is building his Church. Pastor, Christ has called you to humbly and faithfully serve his Bride as he writes her story. You and I get to be part of that story, but it's not our story. Shepherd in humility by looking to the faithfulness of those who have come before you.

ACTION STEPS

1. Which areas of your ministry do you believe could most benefit from historical inquiry? Create a list and develop a timeline for exploring each item listed.

2. Develop a yearlong reading plan to begin engaging some of the recommended resources throughout this book.

3. Subscribe to publications that address both pastoral ministry and church history. I'd recommend the online and print publications of 9Marks, For the Church, and Between the Times.

4. Model for your congregation an appreciation for and the value of our forebears in faith.

REFLECTION QUESTIONS

1. What are the dangers of neglecting church history?

2. How does the past help better prepare us to handle the present and future?

3. Why should your church members know church history?

RECOMMENDED READING:
WHERE TO BEGIN

Historical studies can be an overwhelming venture. To help you find good starting points, I have prepared a list of church history resources, broken into four categories: general church history, the early church, the Reformation, and American church history. I have also organized each category according to reading difficulty (beginner, intermediate, and advanced) along with several primary sources.

GENERAL HISTORY

If you desire to build your library with books that outline church history, these resources would be great for you.

Beginner

Earle E. Cairns, *Christianity Through the Centuries*, 2nd ed. (Grand Rapids: Zondervan, 1981).

Jonathan Hill, *Zondervan Handbook to the History of Christianity* (Grand Rapids: Zondervan, 2006).

Mark A. Noll, *Turning Points: Decisive Moments in the History of Christianity*, 3rd ed. (Grand Rapids, MI: Baker Academic, 2012).

Bruce L. Shelley, *Church History in Plain Language* (Nashville: Thomas Nelson, 1995).

Intermediate

Justo L. Gonzalez, *The Story of Christianity*, 2 vols., rev. ed. (New York: HarperOne, 2010).

Everett Ferguson, *Church History: Volume One; From Christ to Pre-Reformation* (Grand Rapids: Zondervan, 2013).

John D. Woodbridge and Frank A. James III, *Church History: Volume Two; From Pre-Reformation to the Present Day* (Grand Rapids: Zondervan, 2013).

Ruth A. Tucker, *Parade of Faith: A Biographical History of the Christian Church* (Grand Rapids: Zondervan, 2011).

Advanced

Kenneth Scott Latourette, *A History of Christianity*, 2 vols. (New York: Harper & Row, 1975).

Mark A. Noll, *From Every Tribe and Nation: A Historian's Discovery of the Global Christian Story* (Grand Rapids: Baker Academic, 2014).

Jaroslav Pelikan, *The Christian Tradition: A History of the Development of Doctrine*, 5 vols. (Chicago: University of Chicago Press, 1971–1989).

EARLY CHURCH HISTORY

One of my favorite areas of study is the early church. Evangelicals are woefully ignorant of the early church. This ignorance is inexcusable.

Beginner

Henry Chadwick, *The Early Church*, rev. ed. (Hammondsworth, UK: Penguin, 1993).

Michael A. G. Haykin, *Rediscovering the Church Fathers: Who They Were and How They Shaped the Church* (Wheaton, IL: Crossway, 2011).

Eusebius, *Church History*; NPNF[2] 1:81–387.

Intermediate

Paul Foster, *Early Christian Thinkers: The Lives and Legacies of Twelve Key Figures* (Downers Grove, IL: IVP Academic, 2010).

Bradley G. Green, *The Shapers of Early Orthodoxy: Engaging with Early and Medieval Theologians* (Downers Grove, IL: IVP Academic, 2010).

Bryan M. Litfin, *Getting to Know the Church Fathers: An Evangelical Introduction* (Grand Rapids: Brazos, 2007).

Advanced

W. H. C. Frend, *The Rise of Christianity* (Philadelphia: Fortress, 1984).

R. P. C. Hanson, *The Search for the Christian Doctrine of God: The Arian Controversy, 318–81* (Grand Rapids: Baker Academic, 2005).

J. N. D. Kelly, *Early Christian Doctrines*, rev. ed. (San Francisco: Harper & Row, 1978).

Primary Sources

Augustine, *On Nature and Grace*; NPNF 5:116–51.

Gregory the Great, *Pastoral Care*; NPNF[2] 12:1–72.

Irenaeus, *Demonstration of the Apostolic Preaching*, trans. Robinson J. Armitage (London: Society of Promoting Christian Knowledge, 1920); accessible online at www.ccel.org and babel.hathitrust.org.

REFORMATION HISTORY

Why do Protestant churches even exist? As knowledge of the Reformation fades from evangelical memory, the reasons for the Protestant break from the Roman Catholic Church have begun to lose their significance. In an effort to reclaim the truths of the Reformation, it would be wise to understand the context of this pivotal moment in church history.

Beginner

Peter Marshall, *The Reformation: A Very Short Introduction* (Oxford: Oxford University Press, 2009).

Stephen J. Nichols, *The Reformation: How a Monk and a Mallet Changed the World* (Wheaton, IL: Crossway, 2007).

Michael Reeves, *The Unquenchable Flame: Discovering the Heart of the Reformation* (Nashville: B&H Academic, 2010).

Intermediate

Timothy George, *The Theology of the Reformers*, rev. ed. (Nashville: B&H Academic, 2013).

Alister McGrath, *Christianity's Dangerous Idea: The Protestant Revolution; A History from the Sixteenth Century to the Twenty-First* (New York: HarperOne, 2007).

James R. Payton, Jr., *Getting the Reformation Wrong: Correcting Some Misunderstandings* (Downers Grove, IL: IVP Academic, 2010).

Advanced

G. R. Evans, *The Roots of the Reformation: Tradition, Emergence and Rupture*, 2nd ed. rev. (Downers Grove: IVP Academic, 2012).

Carter Lindberg, *The European Reformations* (Malden, MA: Wiley-Blackwell, 2010).

Steven Ozment, *The Age of Reform (1250–1550): An Intellectual and Religious History of Late Medieval and Reformation Europe* (New Haven, CT: Yale University Press, 1980).

Primary Sources

John Calvin, *Institutes of the Christian Religion*, ed. John T. McNeill, trans. Ford Lewis Battles, 2 vols. (Philadelphia: Westminster, 1960). Read with his commentaries, *Calvin's Commentaries*, 46 vols. (Edinburgh: Calvin Translation Society, 1843–1855); available online at www.ccel.org and www.archive.org.

John Donne, *The Sermons of John Donne*, 10 vols., eds. George R. Potter and Evelyn M. Simpson (Berkeley: University of California Press, 1953-1962).

Desiderius Erasmus, *The Praise of Folly*, trans. Clarence H. Miller (New Haven, CT: Yale University Press, 1979).

Martin Luther, *Invocavit Sermons* (1522), in *Luther's Works*, 82 vols. projected (St. Louis: Concordia; Philadelphia: Fortress, 1955-1982, 2009-), 51:67–100; and "Short Instruction: What Should Be Sought and Expected in the Gospels," 75:7–12.

AMERICAN CHURCH HISTORY

The story of the church in America is filled with twists and turns. Debates have and continue to rage over whether America is (or ever was) a Christian nation. Understanding the rise of American religious freedom and the varying influences on the American church is vital to a healthy view of the church.

Beginner

Daryl C. Cornett, ed., *Christian America? Perspectives on Our Religious Heritage* (Nashville: B&H Academic, 2011).

David L. Holmes, *The Faiths of the Founding Fathers* (Oxford: Oxford University Press, 2006).

Douglas A. Sweeney, *The American Evangelical Story: A History of the Movement* (Grand Rapids: Baker Academic, 2005).

Intermediate

Sydney E. Ahlstrom, *A Religious History of the American People* (New Haven, CT: Yale University Press, 1972).

Edwin S. Gaustad, *A Religious History of America* (San Francisco: Harper & Row, 1990).

Mark A. Noll, *A History of Christianity in the United States and Canada* (Grand Rapids: Eerdmans, 1992).

Advanced

D. G. Hart, ed., *Reckoning with the Past: Historical Essays on American Evangelicalism from the Institute for the Study of American Evangelicals* (Grand Rapids: Baker Books, 1995).

Thomas S. Kidd, *God of Liberty: A Religious History of the American Revolution* (New York: Basic Books, 2010).

George M. Marsden, *Fundamentalism and American Culture* (New York: Oxford University Press, 2006).

Mark Noll, *America's God: From Jonathan Edwards to Abraham Lincoln* (Oxford: Oxford University Press, 2005).

Primary Sources

Jonathan Edwards, *Freedom of the Will* (1754), ed. Paul Ramsey (New Haven, CT: Yale University Press, 1957); accessible online at edwards.yale.edu.

A. A. Hodge and B. B. Warfield, *Inspiration* (Grand Rapids: Baker, 1979).

J. Gresham Machen, *Christianity and Liberalism* (Grand Rapids: Eerdmans, 1923).

APPENDIX 1

FREQUENTLY ASKED QUESTIONS

In my time as a pastor, I have been asked difficult questions that require knowledge of church history. In this appendix I supply short, memorable answers and explanations to three questions you will likely be asked during your ministry.

WHAT HAPPENED AT THE COUNCIL OF NICAEA?

Thanks to *The Da Vinci Code* and nearly every anti-Christian conspiracy theory propagated on the internet, many people attach dark and sinister events to the convocation of the Council of Nicaea (325). But what really led to the council's assembly? And what took place?

Before the Nicene Council, Arius began to teach that Jesus was a creature and not the eternal Son of God (see chapter 2). He described Jesus as having a similar substance (*homoiousios*) to the Father. As Arius' influence increased, so did the need to address his theology in a public and authoritative fashion. The council focused on how to reaffirm the orthodox understanding of the Godhead and to clarify how they talked about the one God in three persons. This way they could more clearly distinguish between orthodoxy and Arius' heterodox teaching. The roughly 300 council fathers overwhelmingly affirmed the historic, orthodox, biblical doctrine of the relationship between the Father and the Son: that they are of the same substance (*homoousios*). Jesus wasn't "voted into deity" at Nicaea; instead, his deity was reaffirmed at Nicaea.

For a much more detailed discussion of Nicaea, see my book *Joseph Smith's Tritheism: The Prophet's Theology in Historical Context, Critiqued* from a Nicene Perspective (Eugene, OR: Wipf & Stock, 2014) and Lewis Ayres, *Nicaea and Its Legacy: An Approach to Fourth-Century Trinitarian Theology* (Oxford: Oxford University Press, 2004).

DID JOHN CALVIN MURDER MICHAEL SERVETUS?

Many blame John Calvin (1509–1564) for the execution of the famed heretic Michael Servetus (d. 1553). Often this ad hominem attack is meant to dismantle some of the more controversial claims of Reformed theology. But what really happened between Calvin and Servetus?

For two decades Calvin and Servetus debated several Christian doctrines, particularly the Trinity, which Servetus denied. Servetus' views caught more than just Calvin's attention. The Catholic Inquisition convicted Servetus of heresy and condemned him to die by execution. (During the early modern era, heresy was considered a soul disease that threatened the whole community unless it was eliminated.) Living as a fugitive, Servetus wrote to Calvin that he was coming to Geneva. Despite Calvin's protest that these unwise travel plans could likely result in Servetus' execution, Servetus came to Geneva. The civil authorities arrested him (it's unclear who informed them). Servetus was tried, found guilty, and executed. Calvin only served as a witness to the content of Servetus' doctrine. After trying to dissuade Servetus from his error, Calvin pleaded—unsuccessfully—for mercy, that Servetus would be executed by sword rather than by fire. Servetus' fate would have been no different in any other city.

For more information, see Bruce Gordon, *Calvin* (New Haven, CT: Yale University Press, 2009), 217–32; and Alister McGrath, *A Life of John Calvin: A Study of John Calvin in the Shaping of Western Culture* (Oxford: Wiley-Blackwell, 1990).

WHEN DID CHRISTIANS BECOME TRINITARIAN?

Frequently, I am asked questions about the origin of the doctrine of the Trinity. The modern church's failure to be robustly Trinitarian in its theology and liturgy seems to have led many to confusion regarding the nature of God. So when was the doctrine of the Trinity "invented"?

You will receive this question at some point and it must be answered in stages. First, the doctrine of the Trinity is not grounded in tradition; it is grounded in Scripture. A pastor must be prepared to provide the scriptural basis for the doctrine before ever engaging in a discussion regarding the historical development of Trinitarian language. Christians have always been Trinitarian, even if they lacked the language necessary to express their Trinitarian theology. Second, you must admit that the earliest Christians, though they taught Trinitarian theology, did not use the term "Trinity." Today we are able to express the doctrine of the Trinity clearly and systematically thanks to precise, clear language developed by the ecumenical councils and church fathers.

After thoroughly navigating the first two issues, you would do well to show how early Christians explained the doctrine of the Trinity (even if they failed to use the word "Trinity"). Prior to 200, Christian theologians like Justin Martyr (100–165), Athenagoras (ca. 133–190), and Irenaeus (d. 202), wrote defenses of Christian monotheism while explaining the Christian worship of the Father, Son, and Holy Spirit. Note that the early theologian Tertullian (ca. 160–230) first coined the term "Trinity" in Latin. Some may be troubled to learn that the word "Trinity" came into usage so long after the close of the New Testament. This should not be an issue. (It falsely assumes that for a concept to exist, there must be a word for that concept. This is often called the word-thing fallacy.) Although some who openly denied the deity of Christ taught Christian monotheism in an anti-Trinitarian fashion, orthodox Christianity has always been distinctly Trinitarian, even if the specific theological language required a period of fine-tuning before becoming common usage. Jesus taught this reality when he gave us the Great Commission (Matt 28:18–20 ESV): "All authority in heaven and on earth has been given to me. Go therefore and make disciples of all nations, baptizing them in the name of the Father and of the Son and of the Holy Spirit, teaching them to observe all that I have commanded you. And behold, I am with you always, to the end of the age."

For more information, see Robert Letham, *The Holy Trinity: In Scripture, History, Theology, and Worship* (Phillipsburg, NJ: P&R, 2004) and Donald Fairbairn, *Life in the Trinity: An Introduction to Theology with the Help of the Church Fathers* (Downers Grove, IL: IVP Academic, 2009).

APPENDIX 2

A GUIDE TO CREEDS, CONFESSIONS, AND CATECHISMS

If, in reading this book, you have become interested in integrating creed or confession recitations into your worship services, or if you would like to begin catechizing your children and new believers of any age, this guide will be helpful. I will briefly describe some potential uses for some of the most accessible creeds, confessions, and catechisms.

CREEDS

The Apostles' Creed

Usage

One of the earliest and shortest creeds from the early church, the Apostles' Creed is an excellent and succinct summary of core Christian beliefs. It would be an especially suitable creed to recite during a series on doctrine, around Christmas or Easter, and through sections of Paul's Epistles that deal with the deity of Christ.

Caution

Depending on your context, some of the language may need to be adjusted to avoid confusion. The most sensational clause seems to be "he descended into hell." The word for "hell" is ambiguous, however, and can also be understood as "the dead" as well as the place where the dead are. In most situations, it is probably best to substitute "the grave" or "the dead" in place of "hell." (See further Calvin's discussion of this issue in his *Institutes* 2.16.8–12.[1]) In addition, the creed uses the phrase "the catholic church," which means the universal church—the church of all Christians at all times. (When in lowercase form, catholic simply means "universal.") So, you may want to substitute "universal" or "Christian" in the place of "catholic" (see * below).

> I believe in God, the Father almighty,
> creator of heaven and earth.
> I believe in Jesus Christ, his only Son, our Lord.
> He was conceived by the power of the Holy Spirit
> and born of the Virgin Mary.
> He suffered under Pontius Pilate,
> was crucified, died and was buried.
> He descended to the dead.
> On the third day he rose again.
> He ascended into heaven,
> and is seated at the right hand of the Father.
> He will come again in glory to judge the living and the dead.
> I believe in the Holy Spirit,
> the holy Christian* church,
> the communion of saints,
> the forgiveness of sins,
> the resurrection of the body,
> and the life everlasting. Amen.

The Nicene Creed

Usage

The Nicene Creed could be used in a similar way to the Apostles' Creed. This creed stands as one of the most (if not the most) influential creeds from the early church. Implementing this creed into your worship gatherings connects contemporary Christians to the ancient faith proclaimed by our forebears.

Caution

If you're a Baptist, you will need to explain the phrase "baptism for the forgiveness of sins." As a Baptist and a church historian, I do not believe that the council fathers at Constantinople in 381—that's when the third article reached its final form—meant that baptism saves sinners. Instead, my research and tradition lead me to believe that they equated obedience in baptism (public profession of faith) with saving faith. If you are willing to publicly profess faith in Christ through baptism, you must genuinely repent of your sins.

> I believe in one God,
> the Father, the Almighty,
> maker of heaven and earth,
> of all that is, seen and unseen.
> I believe in one Lord, Jesus Christ,
> the only Son of God,
> eternally begotten of the Father,
> God from God, Light from Light,
> true God from true God,
> begotten, not made,
> of one Being with the Father.
> Through him all things were made.
> For us and for our salvation
> he came down from heaven:
> by the power of the holy Spirit
> he became incarnate from the Virgin Mary,
> and was made man.
> For our sake he was crucified under Pontius Pilate;
> he suffered death and was buried.
> On the third day he rose again
> in accordance with the Scriptures;
> he ascended into heaven
> and is seated at the right hand of the Father.
> He will come again in glory to judge the living and the dead,
> and his kingdom will have no end.
> I believe in the Holy Spirit, the Lord, the giver of life,
> who proceeds from the Father and the Son.
> With the Father and the Son he is worshiped and glorified.
> He has spoken through the prophets.

I believe in one holy Christian* and apostolic church.
I acknowledge one baptism for the forgiveness of sins.
I look for the resurrection of the dead,
and the life of the world to come. Amen.

CONFESSIONS

These detailed summaries of Christian doctrine serve as a manual for the core doctrinal commitments of a theological tradition. Two of the most widely used confessions of faith are the 1689 London Baptist Confession and the Reformed Westminster Confession of Faith (1647). Incorporating your theological tradition's confessional statements into worship services will grow your congregation's theological maturity.

At Redeemer Church, for example, we have recited statements on salvation, the deity of Christ, and the resurrection from the Abstract Principles (1858) and the Baptist Faith and Message (2000).

CATECHISMS

While there are numerous catechisms to choose from, I would like to focus on two that we use in our church.

The New City Catechism

This is a great catechism for the entire family. It is available as an app for your smartphone or tablet. It has settings for both adult and children. A brief video clip explains each question and answer. These videos include Christian pastors and theologians like Timothy Keller and D. A. Carson. In addition, each question includes a brief commentary and memory verse. I deeply appreciate how ecumenical this catechism is. Published by The Gospel Coalition, it reflects the shared beliefs of a variety of traditions. I highly recommend that you promote this catechism in your church.

Truth and Grace Memory Books

This series of catechisms is published by Founders Press and edited by Tom Ascol.[2] These books are explicitly Baptist. There are three booklets in the series, with content increasing in complexity from the first to third booklet. This is a catechism that will grow with your children. Each booklet provides a plan for Scripture memory, catechism questions, and even related hymns. These books help our congregation benefit from the rich traditions of worship.

There are many other catechisms, including the Shorter and Longer Westminster Catechisms, The Heidelberg Catechism, Luther's Small Catechism, and *Teaching Truth and Training Hearts.*[3]

NOTES

Chapter 1: Back to the Future

1. These works are available online at www.ccel.org.

Chapter 2: Creed and Creeds

1. For the text of the Apostles' Creed and the Nicene Creed, see Appendix 2. The Athanasian Creed is another honored creed in the church's history.
2. Kevin P. Emmert, "New Poll Finds Evangelicals' Favorite Heresies," *Christianity Today*, October 28, 2014; accessed online at www.christianitytoday. com/ct/2014/october-web-only/new-poll-finds-evangelicals-favorite-heresies.html.
3. Irenaeus (d. 202) compares the relationship between Scripture and the creeds to a mosaic of a king, see Irenaeus, *Against Heretics*, 1.8.1; ANF 1:326.

Chapter 3: Imitating Christ

1. *Apostolic Tradition* 17.1.
2. *Apostolic Tradition* 15.1; *Apostolic Constitutions* 7.3.39; *Apostolic Tradition* 16.2. *Apostolic Constitutions* is a fourth-century collection of documents that are largely unrelated except for their common theme on spiritual disciplines. *Apostolic Tradition* is generally associated with Hippolytus of Rome; it is believed to have been written shortly after 200. English translations of both texts are available online at www.newadvent.org/fathers/0715.htm and www.earlychristianwritings.com/hippolytus.html, respectively.
3. Michael Wilkins, *Following the Master: Discipleship in the Steps of Jesus* (Grand Rapids: Zondervan, 1992), 313–27.
4. *I Clement* 14:1; 35:5; 40:4; 35:5 (ANF 1:8, 14, 16, 14).
5. *I Clement* 38 (ANF 1:15).
6. Polycarp, *Epistle to the Philippians* 4 (ANF 1:34). Polycarp states that this instruction should happen in the following relationships: husbands to wives, parents to children, the church to widows, and the church to "all others."
7. *Epistle to Diognetus* 11 (ANF 1:29).
8. Edward Smither, *Augustine as Mentor* (Nashville: B&H Academic, 2008), 12.
9. Smither, *Augustine as Mentor*, 134–36.

10. Smither, *Augustine as Mentor*, 147.
11. Smither, *Augustine as Mentor*, 134.
12. See Charles Spurgeon, *Lectures to My Students* (Peabody, MA: Hendrickson, 2010).
13. John Calvin, *Institutes of the Christian Religion*, ed. John T. McNeill, trans. Ford Lewis Battles, 2 vols. (Philadelphia: Westminster, 1960), 2:1460–61 (4.19.13).
14. Sally Lloyd-Jones, *The Jesus Storybook Bible: Every Story Whispers his Name* (Grand Rapids: Zonderkids, 2007).
15. Joel Beeke and Mark Jones, *A Puritan Theology* (Grand Rapids: Reformation Heritage Books, 2012), 964.

Chapter 4: Preaching and the Cultural Drift

1. Robert P. Jones, Daniel Cox, and Thomas Banchoff, *A Generation in Transition: Religion, Values, and Politics among College-Age Millennials; Findings from the 2012 Millennial Values Survey* (Washington, DC: Public Religion Research Institute, 2012); accessed online at publicreligion.org/site/wp-content/uploads/2012/04/Millennials-Survey-Report.pdf.
2. William Edgar, *Reasons of the Heart: Recovering Christian Persuasion* (Phillipsburg, NJ: P&R Publishing, 2003), 12.
3. John Broadus, *A Treatise on the Preparation and Delivery of Sermons* (Louisville, KY: The Southern Baptist Theological Seminary, 2012), 99–100.
4. Tertullian, *Prescription Against Heretics* 7; ANF 3:246.
5. Tertullian, *Apology* 21; ANF 3:33–36.
6. Augustine, *On Christian Doctrine* 4.2; NPNF 2:575.
7. Martin Luther, *Defense of the Translation of the Psalms* (1531), in *Luther's Works*, 82 vols. projected (St. Louis: Concordia; Philadelphia: Fortress, 1955–1986; 2009–), 35:213.
8. A. Skevington Wood, *Captive to the Word: Martin Luther, Doctor of Sacred Scripture* (Exeter, UK: Paternoster, 1969), 85–94.
9. Francis A. Schaeffer, *Escape From Reason* (Downers Grove, IL: InterVarsity Press, 2006), 120.
10. Justin Martyr, *Second Apology* 2; ANF 1:88–89.

Chapter 5: Christians and Culture

1. Kenneth Scott Latourette, *A History of Christianity*, 2 vols. (New York: Harper & Row, 1975), 1:81–82.
2. Augustine, *City of God*, 8.4; NPNF 2:146–47.
3. Augustine, *City of God*, 4; NPNF 2:64–83.
4. Augustine, *City of God*, 2.4; NPNF 2:24–25.
5. Anthony Kenny, ed., *The Oxford History of Western Philosophy* (Oxford: Oxford University Press, 1994), 57–59.
6. Bruce Riley Ashford, *Every Square Inch: An Introduction to Cultural Engagement for Christians* (Bellingham, WA: Lexham Press, 2015), 53.
7. George M. Marsden, *Fundamentalism and American Culture* (Oxford: Oxford University Press, 2006), 22–24.
8. Marsden, *Fundamentalism and American Culture*, 66–68.

9. Francis A. Schaeffer, *How Should We Then Live?: The Rise and Decline of Western Thought and Culture* (Wheaton, IL: Crossway, 2005), 245–52.
10. Schaeffer, *How Should We Then Live?*, 254.

Chapter 6: Yesterday, Today Was the Future

1. John Calvin, *Institutes of the Christian Religion*, ed. John T. McNeill, trans. Ford Lewis Battles, 2 vols. (Philadelphia: Westminster, 1960), 2:1156–57 (4.8.9).
2. From the second article of the Nicene Creed.

Appendix 2: A Guide to Creeds, Confessions, and Catechisms

1. John Calvin, *Institutes of the Christian Religion*, 1:512–20.
2. Tom Ascol, ed., *Truth and Grace Memory Books*, 3 vols., (Cape Coral, FL: Founders Press, 2000).
3. The Westminster and Heidelberg Catechisms are available in various print editions, as well as online at www.reformed.org/documents; so also Luther's Small Catechism, bookofconcord.org; Tom J. Nettles, ed., *Teaching Truth and Training Hearts* (Amityville, NY: Calvary, 1998).

ABBREVIATIONS

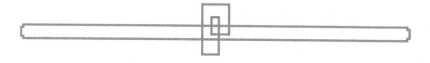

ANF   The Ante-Nicene Fathers. 10 vols. Edited by Alexander Roberts and James Donaldson. Buffalo, NY: Christian Literature, 1885–1896. Available online at www.ccel.org.

NPNF A Select Library of the Nicene and Post-Nicene Fathers of the Christian Church. 28 vols. in two series (NPNF; NPNF²). Edited by Philip Schaff et al. Buffalo, NY: Christian Literature, 1887–1894. Available online at www.ccel.org.

BIBLIOGRAPHY

Ahlstrom, Sydney E. *A Religious History of the American People*. New Haven, CT: Yale University Press, 1972.

Akin, Daniel. *How to Build a Theological Library*. 2013. Accessed online at www.danielakin.com.

Ancient Christian Commentary on Scripture. 29 vols. Edited by Thomas C. Oden. Downers Grove, IL: InterVarsity Press, 1998–2009.

Ancient Christian Texts. Edited by Thomas C. Oden and Gerald L. Bray. Downers Grove, IL: IVP Academic, 2009–.

Ashford, Bruce Riley. *Every Square Inch: An Introduction to Cultural Engagement for Christians*. Bellingham, WA: Lexham Press, 2015.

Ascol, Tom, ed., *Truth and Grace Memory Books*. 3 vols. Cape Coral, FL: Founders Press, 2000.

Ayres, Lewis. *Nicaea and its Legacy: An Approach to Fourth-Century Trinitarian Theology*. Oxford: Oxford University Press, 2004.

Beeke, Joel, and Mark Jones. *A Puritan Theology*. Grand Rapids: Reformation Heritage Books, 2012.

Broadus, John. *A Treatise On the Preparation and Delivery of Sermons*. Louisville, KY: The Southern Baptist Theological Seminary, 2012.

Cairns, Earle E. *Christianity Through the Centuries*. 2nd ed. Grand Rapids: Zondervan, 1981.

Calvin, John. *Institutes of the Christian Religion*. Edited by John T. McNeill. Translated by Ford Lewis Battles. 2 vols. Philadelphia: Westminster, 1960.

Chadwick, Henry. *The Early Church*. Rev. ed. Hammondsworth, UK: Penguin, 1993.

Chester, Tim. *The Apostles' Creed*. Surrey, UK: The Good Book Company, 2006.

Chester, Tim, and Steve Timmis. *Total Church: A Radical Reshaping around Gospel and Community*. Wheaton, IL: Crossway, 2008.

Cornett, Daryl C., ed. *Christian America? Perspectives on Our Religious Heritage*. Nashville: B&H Academic, 2011.

Crouch, Andy. *Culture Making: Recovering Our Creative Calling*. Downers Grove, IL: InterVarsity Press, 2009.

Donne, John. *The Sermons of John Donne*. 10 vols. Edited by George R. Potter and Evelyn M. Simpson. Berkeley: University of California Press, 1953–1962.

Duriez, Colin. *Francis Schaeffer: An Authentic Life*. Wheaton, IL: Crossway, 2008.

Edgar, William. *Reasons of the Heart: Recovering Christian Persuasion*. Phillipsburg, NJ: P&R Publishing, 2003.

Edwards, Jonathan. *Freedom of the Will* (1754). Edited by Paul Ramsey. New Haven, CT: Yale University Press, 1957.

Emmert, Kevin P. "New Poll Finds Evangelicals' Favorite Heresies." *Christianity Today*, October 28, 2014. Accessed online at www.christianitytoday.com/ct/2014/october-web-only/new-poll-finds-evangelicals-favorite-heresies.html.

Erasmus, Desiderius. *The Praise of Folly*. Translated by Clarence H. Miller. New Haven, CT: Yale University Press, 1979.

Evans, G. R. *The Roots of the Reformation: Tradition, Emergence and Rupture*. 2nd ed. rev. Downers Grove: IVP Academic, 2012.

Fairbairn, Donald. *Life in the Trinity: An Introduction to Theology with the Help of the Church Fathers*. Downers Grove, IL: IVP Academic, 2009.

Ferguson, Everett. *Church History: Volume One; From Christ to Pre-Reformation*. Grand Rapids: Zondervan, 2013.

Foster, Paul *Early Christian Thinkers: The Lives and Legacies of Twelve Key Figures*. Downers Grove, IL: IVP Academic, 2010.

Frend, W. H. C. *The Rise of Christianity*. Philadelphia: Fortress, 1984.

Gaustad, Edwin S. *A Religious History of America*. San Francisco: Harper & Row, 1990.

George, Timothy. *The Theology of the Reformers*. Rev. ed. Nashville: B&H Academic, 2013.

Gonzalez, Justo L. *The Story of Christianity*. 2 vols. Rev. ed. New York: HarperOne, 2010.

Gordon, Bruce. *Calvin*. New Haven, CT: Yale University Press, 2009.

Green, Bradley G. *The Shapers of Early Orthodoxy: Engaging with Early and Medieval Theologians.* Downers Grove, IL: IVP Academic, 2010.

Hannah, John D. *The Kregel Pictorial Guide to Church History.* 6 vols. Grand Rapids: Kregel, 2001–2011.

Hanson, R. P. C. *The Search for the Christian Doctrine of God: The Arian Controversy, 318–81.* Grand Rapids: Baker Academic, 2005.

Hart, D. G., ed., *Reckoning with the Past: Historical Essays on American Evangelicalism from the Institute for the Study of American Evangelicals.* Grand Rapids: Baker Books, 1995.

Hartman, Dayton. *Joseph Smith's Tritheism: The Prophet's Theology in Historical Context, Critiqued from a Nicene Perspective.* Eugene, OR: Wipf & Stock, 2014.

Haykin, Michael A. G. *Rediscovering the Church Fathers: Who They Were and How They Shaped the Church.* Wheaton, IL: Crossway, 2011.

Hill, Jonathan. *Zondervan Handbook to the History of Christianity.* Grand Rapids: Zondervan, 2006.

Hodge, A. A., and B. B. Warfield. *Inspiration.* Grand Rapids: Baker, 1979.

Holcomb, Justin S. *Know the Creeds and Councils.* Grand Rapids: Zondervan, 2014.

Holmes, David L. *The Faiths of the Founding Fathers.* Oxford: Oxford University Press, 2006.

House, Paul R. *Bonhoeffer's Seminary Vision: A Case for Costly Discipleship and Life Together.* Wheaton, IL: Crossway, 2015.

Jones, Robert P., Daniel Cox, and Thomas Banchoff. *A Generation in Transition: Religion, Values, and Politics among College-Age Millennials; Findings from the 2012 Millennial Values Survey.* Washington, DC: Public Religion Research Institute, 2012. Accessed online at publicreligion.org/site/wp-content/uploads/2012/04/Millennials-Survey-Report.pdf

Keller, Timothy. *Preaching: Communicating Faith in an Age of Skepticism.* New York: Viking Press, 2015.

Kelly, J. N. D. *Early Christian Doctrines.* Rev. ed. San Francisco: Harper & Row, 1978.

Kenny, Anthony, ed. *The Oxford History of Western Philosophy.* Oxford: Oxford University Press, 1994.

Kidd, Thomas S. *God of Liberty: A Religious History of the American Revolution.* New York: Basic Books, 2010.

Latourette, Kenneth Scott. *A History of Christianity*. 2 vols. New York: Harper & Row, 1975.

Letham, Robert. *The Holy Trinity: In Scripture, History, Theology, and Worship*. Phillipsburg, NJ: P&R, 2004.

Lindberg, Carter. *The European Reformations*. Malden, MA: Wiley-Blackwell, 2010.

Litfin, Bryan M. *Getting to Know the Church Fathers: An Evangelical Introduction*. Grand Rapids: Brazos, 2007.

Lloyd-Jones, Sally. *The Jesus Storybook Bible: Every Story Whispers His Name*. Grand Rapids: Zonderkids, 2007.

Luther, Martin. *Luther's Works*. 82 vols. projected. St. Louis: Concordia; Philadelphia: Fortress, 1955–1982, 2009–.

Machen, J. Gresham. *Christianity and Liberalism*. Grand Rapids: Eerdmans, 1923.

Marsden, George M. *Fundamentalism and American Culture*. Oxford: Oxford University Press, 2006.

Marshall, Peter. *The Reformation: A Very Short Introduction*. Oxford: Oxford University Press, 2009.

McGrath, Alister. *A Life of John Calvin: A Study of John Calvin in the Shaping of Western Culture*. Oxford: Wiley-Blackwell, 1990.

_____. *Christianity's Dangerous Idea: The Protestant Revolution; A History from the Sixteenth Century to the Twenty-First*. New York: HarperOne, 2007.

_____. *Heresy: A History of Defending the Truth*. New York: HarperOne, 2009.

Merida, Tony. *Faithful Preaching: Declaring Scripture with Responsibility, Passion, and Authority*. Nashville: B&H Academic, 2009.

Mouw, Richard. *Abraham Kuyper: A Short and Personal Introduction*. Grand Rapids: Eerdmans, 2011.

Nettles, Tom J., ed., *Teaching Truth and Training Hearts*. Amityville, NY: Calvary, 1998.

Nichols, Stephen J. *The Reformation: How a Monk and a Mallet Changed the World*. Wheaton, IL: Crossway, 2007.

Noll, Mark A. *A History of Christianity in the United States and Canada*. Grand Rapids: Eerdmans, 1992.

_____. *America's God: From Jonathan Edwards to Abraham Lincoln*. Oxford: Oxford University Press, 2005.

_____. *Turning Points: Decisive Moments in the History of Christianity.* Grand Rapids: Baker Academic, 2012.

_____. *From Every Tribe and Nation: A Historian's Discovery of the Global Christian Story.* Grand Rapids: Baker Academic, 2014.

Ozment, Steven. *The Age of Reform (1250–1550): An Intellectual and Religious History of Late Medieval and Reformation Europe.* New Haven, CT: Yale University Press, 1980.

Packer, J. I. *Affirming the Apostles' Creed.* Wheaton, IL: Crossway, 2008.

Payton, James R., Jr. *Getting the Reformation Wrong: Correcting Some Misunderstandings.* Downers Grove, IL: IVP Academic, 2010.

Pelikan, Jaroslav. *The Christian Tradition: A History of the Development of Doctrine.* 5 vols. Chicago: University of Chicago Press, 1971–1989.

Quash, Ben, and Michael Ward, eds. *Heresies and How to Avoid Them: Why It Matters What Christians Believe.* London: SPCK, 2007.

Rea, Robert F. *Why Church History Matters: An Invitation to Love and Learn from Our Past.* Downers Grove, IL: InterVarsity Press, 2014.

Reeves, Michael. *The Unquenchable Flame: Discovering the Heart of the Reformation.* Nashville: B&H Academic, 2010.

Reformation Commentary on Scripture. 28 vols. projected. Edited by Timothy George and Scott M. Manetsch. Downers Grove, IL: IVP Academic, 2011–.

Schaeffer, Francis A. *How Should We Then Live?: The Rise and Decline of Western Thought and Culture.* Wheaton, IL: Crossway, 2005.

_____. *Escape from Reason.* Downers Grove, IL: InterVarsity Press, 2006.

Shelley, Bruce L. *Church History in Plain Language.* Nashville: Thomas Nelson, 1995.

Smither, Edward L. *Augustine as Mentor: A Model for Preparing Spiritual Leaders.* Nashville: B&H Academic, 2008.

Spurgeon, Charles. *Lectures to My Students.* Peabody, MA: Hendrickson, 2010.

Sweeney, Douglas A. *The American Evangelical Story: A History of the Movement.* Grand Rapids: Baker Academic, 2005.

Trueman, Carl R. *The Creedal Imperative.* Wheaton, IL: Crossway, 2012.

Tucker, Ruth. *Parade of Faith: A Biographical History of the Christian Church.* Grand Rapids: Zondervan, 2011.

Vanderstelt, Jeff. *Saturate: Being Disciples of Jesus in the Everyday Stuff of Life.* Wheaton, IL: Crossway, 2015.

Walton, Robert C. *Chronological and Background Charts of Church History.* Rev. ed. Grand Rapids: Zondervan, 2005.

Wilkins, Michael. *Following the Master: Discipleship in the Steps of Jesus.* Grand Rapids: Zondervan, 1992.

Wood, A. Skevington. *Captive to the Word: Martin Luther, Doctor of Sacred Scripture.* Exeter, UK: Paternoster, 1969.

Woodbridge, John D., and Frank A. James III. *Church History: Volume Two; From Pre-Reformation to the Present Day.* Grand Rapids: Zondervan, 2013.

Yarhouse, Mark A. *Understanding Gender Dysphoria.* Downers Grove, IL: IVP Academic, 2015.

SUBJECT AND AUTHOR INDEX

A

Abstract Principles, The (SBC), 18, 73
adoptionism, 15
Ahlstrom, Sydney E., 65
Akin, Daniel, 11
anarchy, cultural, 51
Apollos, and apologetics, 38
apologetics, 38-41
Apostles' Creed, 19-20, 70-71
Arianism, 4
Aristotle, 38
Arius, 14-15, 67
art, 42, 52-53
Ascol, Tom, 73
Ashford, Bruce Riley, 46-49, 54
Athanasian Creed, 20
Athenagoras, 69
Augustine, 3, 26-28, 37, 47-48, 51-53, 58, 63
Ayres, Lewis, 14, 68

B

Back to the Future, 3-4
baptism, in the Nicene Creed, 71-72
Baptist Faith and Message (SBC), 18, 73
Baptists
    and catechisms, 20, 73-74

confessions of, 18
    and polity, 5-6
Beecher, Henry Ward, 49
BFM2000. See *Baptist Faith and Message*
Bray, Gerald L., 41
Broadus, John, 35, 44

C

Cairns, Earle E., 61
Calvin, John, 20, 28-29, 48, 51, 56-58, 64, 68-71
Carson, D. A., 73
Catechism for Babes, or Little Ones, A (Jesseynde), 20
catechisms, 20, 73-74
    and discipling children, 28-30
"catholic," in the Apostles' Creed, 71
Chadwick, Henry, 62
Chester, Tim, 22, 32
children, discipleship of, 28-30
Christ, as the hope, 58-59
Christology, controversies of, 4-5, 14-15, 67-68
chronological snobbery, 2, 7, 57
church, early, and discipleship, 24-26
Church, the, and humility, 58

SCRIPTURE INDEX

Old Testament

New Testament